Pucking My Fake Fiancé

AN ENEMIES TO LOVERS SMALL TOWN ROMANCE

LIVVY STONE

Join Livvy Stone's Readers' Circle!

Snag *thousands* of freebies, bargains and sneak peeks, get the scoop on the latest releases, and be the first to dive into upcoming stories. Oh, and did we mention your welcome gift? Say hello to 'Pucking My Brother's Best Friend,' Livvy's FREE eBook crafted just for you!

Scan this QR code to join and download your free book!

Scan me

Contents

1

Hailey

SUMMER, TEN YEARS AGO

"I SWEAR, LUCY, MAX freaking Decker's ego must be the size of Cedarwood's hockey rink," I grumble, gripping my plastic cup a bit too tightly. The bass from the house party thumps against the walls, drowning in a sea of red solo cups and teen hormones. "Did you see him at practice today? Acts like he owns the place."

Lucy Marks, my ride-or-die since sandbox days, takes a languid sip of her drink, smirking. "You know, for someone who claims to loathe our resident Hockey God, you sure obsess over him a lot. And besides, doesn't it feel good to get out of the house for once and go to an actual party instead of staying at home with Dostoevsky or whatever brainy book you're reading these days?"

Truth be told, being at home with some tea and a good book—my usual Friday night routine once studying is done—still sounds pretty good. But my mind caught on a particular word Hailey had used.

I huff, rolling my eyes. "Obsess? Please. I can't help but hear about Max's latest 'amazing' goal or how he 'heroically' assisted Mrs. Peterson with her groceries."

Lucy waggles her eyebrows, leaning in. "Just jealous he lent Mrs. Peterson a hand instead of lending you... other things."

My cheeks flame, and I nearly choke on my drink. "Lucy! I wouldn't want him anywhere near me. Especially not for... 'other things.'"

Her laughter fills the air, warm and infectious. "Okay, okay. I believe you. Sort of."

Taking a defiant swig, I grumble, "He's a cocky, self-centered jerk."

"But?" she prods.

"There's no 'but'!"

Lucy pokes my side, making me squirm. "Admit it. He's all that, but Max Decker is also scorchingly hot."

My heart races at the mere mention of Max and his completely unfair good looks.

Deep breaths, Hailey.

"Okay, fine," I admit grudgingly, "From a purely objective standpoint, he's... 'slightly' attractive."

"'Slightly' attractive?" Lucy practically cackles. "Honey, if he's just 'slightly,' then I'm Taylor Swift."

"Alright, alright!" I groan. "Yes, he's good-looking. Happy now?"

Her eyes twinkle mischievously. "Delighted."

Lucy's gaze then drifts around the grand room, taking in the lavish surroundings. "Speaking of Decker, can you believe this place? It's like something out of a movie."

I follow her gaze, my eyes widening at the expanse of the luxurious mansion. "It's insane. I can't believe his parents are cool with him throwing a party like this. It's like they handed him the keys to a castle and said, 'Go wild, kid.'"

Lucy nods, sipping her drink. "Max Decker, Cedarwood's prince in his palace. Must be nice to have this kind of freedom."

I can't help but feel a twinge of something that feels a lot like envy. "Yeah, 'nice' is one word for it. Must be convenient to have a place where you can be the center of attention without even trying."

Lucy chuckles, nudging me playfully. "Come on, let's go explore the palace. Maybe we'll stumble upon the royal throne room." Her grin is infectious, and despite my misgivings about Max, I find myself being swept up in the excitement of the moment.

Before we can get moving, however, a familiar shadow descends upon us.

"Mind if I hang with you ladies?" That deep, teasing voice can only belong to one person.

My heart doesn't just skip a beat—it leaps out of my chest. Not in the delightful rom-com way, more like the 'I've just admitted the school heartthrob is a total babe and he's now inches away' way.

I slowly turn, coming face-to-face with the very subject of our gossip.

Every time I see Max Decker, it's like the universe is playing some cruel joke on me. It's as if it grabbed every heartthrob from every movie and combined them into this... god of Cedarwood High.

Dark, tousled hair that looks like he's just rolled out of bed—or maybe rolled out of someone else's, if the rumors are true. Those stormy, blue eyes, filled with mischief and secrets, look like they've been crafted to make any girl's insides tangle. And the smirk! Good lord, that smirk could melt glaciers—or a hockey rink.

Lucy, seemingly sensing an opportunity for mischief, springs up. "I'll let you two chat. Catch you later, Hailey!" With a wicked wink she vanishes into the crowd, leaving me in the glaring spotlight with Max.

Great. Just great.

Summoning my sass, I tilt my chin up. "What do you want, Decker?"

His eyes gleam with mischief. "Just thought I'd keep you company. Unless you'd rather continue discussing me behind my back?"

Max leans closer, his presence both overwhelming and tantalizing. The scent of him, some intoxicating mix of wood and fresh winter air, teases my senses. A hint of his cologne mingles with the other party smells.

I fight back the urge to take a step back, to create some distance. "We were just chatting," I respond, attempting nonchalance. "Not everything revolves around you, you know."

He chuckles, a rich sound that I hate for finding so attractive. "Based on what I just heard, it seems a lot of your conversation tonight revolved around me." Max raises an eyebrow, and that smirk grows ever so slightly.

My cheeks burn, and I mentally curse Lucy for her impeccable timing. "It was mere observation, Decker. Don't get ahead of yourself."

Still, he inches closer, now merely a breath away. It's distracting, feeling his warmth, hearing the soft rhythm of his breathing. The thrum of the party fades to the background, replaced by this charged atmosphere between us.

"Why are you here, Max?" I finally ask, my voice low and filled with both irritation and reluctant interest.

His blue eyes search mine for a moment, as if he's looking for something he can't quite pinpoint. "Have you ever considered that maybe I like the challenge of getting under your skin?"

"Quite an aim for high school," I retort, trying to sound unimpressed. But my heartbeat betrays me, pulsing rapidly.

He smirks. "Well, high school's all about setting the foundation for the future, isn't it?" His eyes take on a playful glint as he leans in a bit closer. "I mean, look at us. I've got the NHL practically drooling over my skills, and you? You're burning the midnight oil, racking up those perfect grades like the good girl you are."

It's classic Max—a tease and a compliment all at once. Is this what all those other girls at school, the ones totally obsessed with him, can't resist? In spite of myself, I can feel it working, having some effect on me... and I kind of hate it and love it at the same time.

I can't help but laugh at his words. A genuine laugh that feels like a release. "Is that why you're here? Building a foundation with me?"

His gaze softens, and for a moment, that notorious confidence seems to waver. "I don't know, Hailey. Maybe I'm curious."

My defenses come up immediately. "About?"

He shrugs, his casual demeanor returning. "What's next for Hailey after Cedarwood? I mean, we're all thinking about it, right? Graduation, future... all that stuff."

I tilt my head, watching him closely. The Max Decker I know doesn't do serious. He's the playboy of Cedarwood High, the hockey star with an ego larger than the rink he plays on. And yet, here he is, attempting genuine conversation.

"Why do you care?" I ask, honestly curious.

He shrugs again, his fingers playing with the edge of his shirt. "Maybe I'm tired of the games. Maybe, just for tonight, I wanted to see if there's more to Hailey Rogers than the fiery glares and sassy comebacks."

I blink, taken aback. We've been rivals for as long as I can remember. Teasing jabs, competitive banter—it's always been our thing. But this... this feels different. "There's a lot you don't know about me, Decker."

His gaze holds mine, and there's an intensity there I've never seen before. "Then show me."

The atmosphere between us is electric, the pull undeniable. Part of me wants to run, to get away from this confusing, magnetic force that is Max Decker. But another part, a part I don't want to admit to, is intrigued.

Max's nearness makes it hard to concentrate, and yet I can't help but glance over his broad shoulder, searching the room for a familiar face. My brother's face.

He catches the movement, eyes narrowing in playful suspicion. "Looking for an escape route?"

"I'm looking for Jake," I correct, not willing to give him the satisfaction of thinking I'd want to escape. Though with the way my heart races and cheeks flush, maybe I do.

Max looks genuinely surprised. "Your brother? Why?"

I fold my arms, leaning back slightly, trying to reclaim some personal space. "Considering the shift in our... dynamic tonight, I think there's a pretty good chance my dear brother—and your best friend—has something to do with it—maybe an elaborate screw-with-Hailey attempt that you both came up with."

He chuckles, the sound rich and deep. It reverberates in the small space between us, the laugh lines around his eyes deepening. God, why did those have to be so attractive? "You think Jake set this up?"

I narrow my eyes, trying to decipher if he's playing games or being genuine. "Wouldn't be the first time you two have joined forces to torment me."

Max leans in, so close that our noses almost touch. The intimacy is both startling and exhilarating. "Believe me, Hailey, if I wanted to corner you at a party, I wouldn't need Jake's help."

My breath catches, and a flurry of butterflies take flight in my stomach. "Is that so?"

"Oh, absolutely." He flashes me that confident, heart-stopping smirk again. "Though," he adds, glancing towards the back door that leads out, "If you're convinced there's some grand conspiracy afoot, maybe we should head to the roof? Less prying eyes and all."

The thought of being alone with Max, especially in such a secluded spot, sends a thrill through me. "Why the roof? Trying to impress me with some grand gesture?"

He shrugs, mischief dancing in his eyes. "Maybe I just want a chance to talk without the entire party eavesdropping. Or maybe I want to show you the stars. Who knows?"

It's ridiculous how tempting he makes it sound. Like an adventure. Like a dare.

Against my better judgment, I nod. "Alright, Decker. Lead the way."

The back door creaks slightly as he pushes it open, revealing a narrow staircase that leads to the roof. Max gestures for me to go first. "Ladies first."

The ascent feels both endless and too short. Once we emerge onto the roof, the night air wraps around us, cool and crisp. The soft glow of party lights from the ground mingles with the starry sky above. The murmur of dozens of conversations blends with the music coming from inside the house. But it's quieter here, peaceful even.

I lean against the railing, looking out over the party. "I still can't believe your parents let you throw parties like this," I say, half in jest[ek1] .

Max's expression shifts, a hint of something more serious flickering in his eyes. "Foster parents," he corrects softly. "And they're not really around much."

I pause, taken aback by his correction and the sudden change in his demeanor. There's a weight in his words that hints at a story I've never heard, a depth to Max Decker I hadn't considered. "Oh, I didn't know," I murmur, unsure of what else to say.

He shrugs, the cocky smile returning as if on cue, but it's half-hearted. "No big deal. They give me space, I keep out of trouble... most of the time."

I can't help but feel there's more he's not saying, layers to Max that aren't part of the public persona. But before I can probe any further, he's back to his usual self.

He winks, leaning in closer. "Besides, who wouldn't want to have the freedom to bring a beautiful girl to a rooftop? Seems like a fair trade to me."

I roll my eyes, but I'm smiling despite myself. "You never miss a beat, do you, Decker?"

He grins, that familiar, easy arrogance back in place. "Never. It's part of my charm." Max walks to the edge, rests his arms on the railing. "So," he says, voice soft, "convinced yet that this isn't a setup?"

I step beside him, the view breathtaking. "Honestly? With you, I'm never quite sure."

He glances over, his gaze intense. "Then let me make things clearer." Without warning, he takes a step closer, eliminating the space between us. His fingers brush against my cheek, sending tingles down my spine.

"Max?" I whisper, my voice shaky.

His lips are inches from mine. "Just a talk, remember?"

Before I can reply, he kisses me—softly, gently. It's a touch filled with promise and questions. And just as quickly as it started, he pulls away, a playful smirk gracing his lips. "Still think Jake put me up to this?"

Lost in the whirlwind of emotions, all I can do is smile weakly. "Not anymore."

With that, we fall back into the kiss. And the moment his lips touch mine, I'm done—total surrender.

Each brush of Max's lips against mine feels like a new discovery. A sweet surrender to a force I can neither resist nor comprehend. The taste of him is intoxicating, a mix of the drink he'd been sipping earlier and something uniquely Max—a flavor bold and daring, just like the man himself.

His arms, strong and unyielding, pull me flush against him. The hard contours of his chest, his muscular arms, every inch of him feels like a fortress. I'm enclosed within it, both protected and prisoner to his raw masculinity.

I gasp slightly when his hands begin their own journey of exploration. The warmth of his fingers as they trail over my waist, my hip, the small of my back. Every touch feels charged, electric. And as his hand drifts lower, caressing places no boy has dared venture before, a mixture of exhilaration and apprehension surges within me.

The undeniable proof of his arousal presses into my thigh, a testament to the passion flaring between us. It's both frightening and thrilling, a tangible sign of Max's desire for me. And yet, with each caress, each shared breath, I feel an odd sense of safety, as if being with him is where I'm meant to be.

But as the kiss deepens, the persistent tug of doubt yanks me back from the brink of absolute abandon. Why now? Why me? The Max Decker, Cedarwood's heartthrob, has never shown this kind of interest before. For all the girls he's been with, none had been anything like me—the one who's always been on the periphery, never quite fitting into his world, the girl who'd rather spend her night at home with a book than at a party.

This sudden intensity, this fervor—it's both overwhelming and perplexing.

But the wheels of thought screech to a halt when Max breaks away, only slightly, his breath ragged, his gaze dark with longing. "Hailey," he murmurs, each syllable filled with a hunger that mirrors my own.

"Max." I can scarcely believe the yearning that hangs on that one, single word.

And then comes the question, delivered with a hint of mischief, yet underpinned by a genuine desire.

"Want to find a bedroom?"

2

Max

THE SECOND THE BEDROOM door slams shut, Hailey's lips find mine, and we're kissing with a ferocity that sets every nerve ending on fire. It's wild, relentless, and damn, I can't believe this is happening.

My best friend's sister? Really?

Really.

Her lips are insistent, tasting of that cherry-flavored drink she'd been sipping all evening. And as she pushes me against the door, all thoughts of where I am and who I'm with start to blur. This is Hailey, Jake's twin, the one girl I should've placed in the 'off-limits' category in my mind. But right now, categories, rules, and everything else fall by the wayside.

I hadn't walked into this party tonight, the last hurrah of our senior year, with a plan to end up here. Seduce my best friend's sister? That's the kind of move that doesn't just break the bro code; it obliterates it. Yet here I am, the magnetic pull between us undeniable, our bodies pressed together, the room heating more and more by the moment.

Breaking away for a mere second, her eyes wide and breath ragged, Hailey speaks. "Max, what are we doing?"

I search her eyes, seeing the same surprise and heat reflected back. My usually quick wit feels just out of grasp, but I can't let her see me falter.

Grinning cheekily, I quip, "I think we're taking the term 'ending senior year with a bang' pretty damn literally." I wink.

Hailey chuckles, a sound that eases the tension, but only slightly. "Always with a joke," she replies, her fingers tracing patterns on my chest.

The weight of the situation dawns on me. This isn't just some fling. This is Hailey. The game has changed, and for the first time in a long while, I'm not sure how to play. Not a familiar feeling when you're a god on the rink and with women.

The intoxicating warmth of our lips meeting is momentarily interrupted by the faint sound of music from downstairs. I recognize the unmistakable opening beats of Gotye's 'Somebody That I Used To Know.'

Even in this heated moment, my inner goofball can't resist. I start singing along, right into our kiss.

"Now and then I think of when we were together..." I half-mumble the words against her lips.

She breaks into a giggle, pulling back for a moment to look at me with amused eyes. "Really? Now?" Hailey laughs, but then joins in, "Like when you said you felt so happy you could die..."

I chuckle, a playful spark in my eyes. She's got a pretty decent voice, even if she's using it to tease me right now.

"Are you trying to tell me something with that choice of lyric?" I ask with mock seriousness.

She gives a mischievous shrug, then in a playfully challenging tone says, "Maybe we should be downstairs dancing to your favorite song?"

Laughing, I roll my eyes. "It's not my favorite song. I'm more of a Zeppelin, Rolling Stones kind of guy." I admit, tapping a quick rhythm on her hip. "But, you've got to admit, it's catchy."

Pulling her closer and letting my voice drop to a sultrier tone, I speak. "And that's a no on the dancing—I'm exactly where I want to be."

She smiles, eyes softening, and then our lips meet again, diving back into the passion we've only just begun to explore.

Hailey stands before me, a vision that momentarily knocks the wind out of my usually unflappable sails. The soft glow from the lamp highlights the gentle curve of her cheekbones, and the intensity of her emerald eyes, framed by long dark lashes, pierce me with a fervor I've never felt before. Her lips, painted a tempting shade of deep red, are slightly parted, her breath coming out in short, ragged intervals.

She wears a black dress, the kind that clings to her in all the right places, highlighting the graceful arch of her back and the soft swell of her hips. The hem dances just above her knees, offering teasing glimpses of her toned legs, which lead to a pair of killer heels that I'm certain have left a trail of broken hearts tonight. Her hair, a cascade of chocolate waves, tumbles down her back like a midnight waterfall.

And as I drink in the sight, I'm hit with a realization that leaves me unsteady: This isn't the usual lustful admiration I feel. This is deeper, rawer, and damn it, far more terrifying.

"You okay there, Decker?" Hailey's voice cuts through my reverie, the edge in her tone unmistakable.

"Yeah. Fine. Better than fine."

She takes a step back, her guard going up. "What is this, Max? Another one of your sick games? Planning to mock me after getting my hopes up or something?" She sighs, shaking her head as if she'd figured it out.

I'm usually quick with a retort, always ready with some cheeky response. But now, seeing the mixture of hope and hurt in her gaze, all I feel is an urge to reassure her, to comfort her, to protect her.

What the hell is going on?

"No," I reply, the sincerity in my voice surprising even me. "Hailey, this isn't a game. Not this time."

She searches my eyes, looking for a hint of deception, but all she finds is genuine intensity. Emboldened, I take a step closer, wrapping one arm around her slender waist, pulling her flush against me.

Without another word, I capture her lips with mine. The kiss is fierce, all-consuming. The kiss deepens, our lips and tongues tangling in a passionate dance. Each moment, each touch, is more intense than the last. The thumping bass and laughter from the party become a distant echo, easily drowned out by the thundering of my own heartbeat and the hitched breaths we share.

Hands roaming, I deftly unzip Hailey's dress, letting it fall to the ground in a whisper of fabric. My eyes travel over her, taking in the sight, and damn if she isn't perfection incarnate. Smooth, creamy skin contrasted by the mismatched set of teal bra and pink panties she has on.

A smirk tugs at my lips. "Planning a fashion show I wasn't aware of?"

She blushes, a rosy hue spreading across her cheeks. "I didn't exactly think someone would be inspecting my underwear tonight," she retorts, playfully slapping my chest.

My laughter fills the room—a genuine, full-throated sound. "Well, if it's any consolation, I think the mismatch makes you even more irresistible."

She hooks her fingers into the hem of my shirt, pulling it upwards. I get the hint, quickly removing it and tossing it aside. My skin tingles under her gaze as she drinks in the sight of me. Years of training and hockey have sculpted my body, and I can tell she's impressed—maybe even a bit overwhelmed. Her eyes trace the contours of my abs, lingering on the V-line that leads further down.

There's a hint of shyness in her eyes—a vulnerability that's both endearing and wildly attractive. It strikes me that while I'm usually the confident one, the roles have somewhat reversed in this scenario. And I find myself loving this flustered, bashful side of Hailey.

Closing the distance between us, I capture her lips once more, the taste of her becoming an addiction I'm all too willing to indulge in. Our bodies gravitate towards the bed, and as we tumble onto the soft sheets, a sense of urgency takes over.

Clothes are discarded, forgotten in heaps on the floor as our hands map out familiar yet uncharted territory. It's a heady mix of discovery and desire—every touch, every caress sending shockwaves of pleasure coursing through us.

The cool sheets of the bed contrast sharply with the heat of our entwined bodies. Hailey's breathing comes out in short, ragged bursts, her wide eyes reflecting a mix of desire and nervousness. I can tell that she's not as seasoned in these intimate moments as I am, but it doesn't matter. In fact, it only makes everything more electrifying. The thrill of exploration, of guiding her, is something I haven't experienced in a long while.

A devilish smile curves my lips as I gently take her hand, guiding it down to the throbbing heat of my arousal. "Touch me," I whisper huskily, intertwining our fingers. "Like this."

I show her the rhythm, the pressure, watching as her face morphs from uncertainty to fascination. The sensation of her soft hand, combined with the rawness of this moment, makes my head spin.

But while I'm teaching her, I'm not about to leave her unattended. My free hand drifts to her inner thighs, my fingers dancing tantalizingly close to where she aches the most. She gasps, her eyes locking onto mine, silently pleading.

I've always prided myself on my bedroom prowess, and I intend to show Hailey just how good I can make her feel. With confident strokes, I explore her, each touch designed to drive her wild. Her responses are pure, unfiltered, the sounds she makes music to my ears. Her inner warmth grips me tightly, her wetness growing with each passing moment I'm inside of her.

It doesn't take long. The combination of the night's events, the anticipation, and my attentive touches has her spiraling quickly. Her grip on me tightens, her body arching as waves of pleasure crash over her.

"Oh... oh my God!" She yells out so loudly that part of me wonders if the whole damn party heard.

And through it all, I can't help but marvel at the raw intimacy of this moment—the connection that binds us, defying time and circumstances.

"That... that was... wow," Hailey stammers out, her voice soft and filled with wonder.

Looking down at her, I can't help but feel a primal urge surging through me. Her skin, flushed and dewy, her chest rising and falling rapidly, her small, pink nipples hard. Damn, she's a sight to behold. It's a heady mix of vulnerability and raw beauty that has my heart racing.

Shifting my position, I move to hover above her, settling between her legs. I can feel the heat of her, the intense desire that resonates between us. My manhood brushes against her, making us both gasp. The anticipation, the tension, it's nearly unbearable.

I lock eyes with her, searching her face. "You sure you're ready for this?"

For a second, her gaze falters, and she looks away.

Something's on her mind.

Just as I'm about to voice my concern, she meets my eyes again, determination clear. "Yeah, Max. I'm ready."

Wasting no time, I fish my wallet out of my pants and pull out a condom, quickly rolling it on. As I position myself at her entrance, I take a deep breath, our gazes never breaking. The initial push has us both gasping, the sensation, the intimacy of the moment overwhelming. It's new territory for both of us in different ways.

She's tight—so tight that it takes me a second to adjust. She winces with pleasure as I move into her, my thickness stretching her out. I know I'm a lot to take, and I push into her slowly, letting her get used to my size. I glance down, the sight of my cock vanishing between her legs turning me on even more. Hailey's nails dig into the thick muscles of my upper back, each push of my manhood bringing out another sharp gasp.

Soon, I'm buried inside of her.

"How does that feel?"

She bites her lip, her chest rising and falling again.

"It's... good."

I grin. "Just good?"

She laughs. "Figures you wouldn't be happy with just good." Her smile vanishes for a moment, replaced by tension as she shifts her hips. She moans with pleasure, grinding herself against me. "Better than good. Fucking amazing."

I laugh. "If I can make the nerd say a swear, I know I'm doing something right."

She playfully swats my shoulder. "Nerd. I ought to teach you a lesson for that one, Decker."

"Eager to be taught."

We kiss again, the twin sensation of her lips against mine and my hardness inside of her driving me wild.

Slowly, I begin to move, our bodies finding a rhythm. The sensation is intense, every nerve ending on fire. The way she feels, the sounds she makes, it all drives me wild. The world outside fades away, and all that matters is the here and now, the connection between us.

Time blurs, the room filled with the sounds of soft moans, whispered encouragements, and the unmistakable rhythm of two bodies becoming one. It's raw, real, and unlike anything I've ever felt before.

The intensity ramps up, every touch, every thrust amplifying the pleasure coursing through us. I can feel Hailey's body tense beneath me, and soon, she's tipping over the edge again.

"Max, please, just-like-that, just-like-that!"

She bucks into me from below, guiding me right where she wants me. I'm thrusting into her hard and fast enough to make her breasts shake and the bed groan underneath us. Each push inside her tightness brings me closer and closer to release.

Not a chance I'm done until she is.

Finally, with one more silent scream, Hailey comes. Her climax sends me spiraling, and in the heated frenzy of the moment, I can't hold back any longer. I groan hard, my cock draining into the condom, pleasure shooting up my length. She's shaking from the intensity of her orgasm, and the sight brings me to another level of arousal.

Moments later, we're side by side, chests heaving, trying to catch our breath. The post-orgasmic haze is thick and palpable. But there's something else, something I can't quite put my finger on. An awkwardness? A realization? The room, which moments ago was filled with sounds of passion, is now eerily quiet.

I turn to look at Hailey, her eyes slightly wide as if she's trying to process everything. There's vulnerability there, a rawness that I've never seen before. And that's when it hits me—maybe, just maybe, I've caught feelings for this girl. This is a foreign territory for me. Feelings? Emotions? Not exactly Max Decker's style.

I want to say something. I know I should say something.

But I can't. I am speechless and overcome by whatever the hell I am feeling.

"You... you OK?" she asks. Hailey's sensing something's wrong.

I don't know what to do.

Before I can dive into that train of thought, my phone buzzes, breaking the silence. A text from Jake.

Dude, where are you? Party's winding down.

Perfect timing, I think, the escape route I didn't know I needed. Pushing aside the strange cocktail of emotions bubbling up, I spring into action.

"Time to go," I say, hopping out of bed and grabbing my scattered clothes. I toss Hailey her dress and underwear, flashing her a roguish grin. "As fun as this was, I think we've crashed this party long enough."

She just stares at me, a mixture of surprise and something I can't quite decipher in her eyes. Without waiting for a response, I pull on my jeans, slip into my shirt, and head for the door.

"Catch you around this summer, maybe."

As soon as I say the words, I realize they came off more flippant than I wanted, like I didn't give a damn about her one way or the other. The truth was, that was the opposite of how I felt in those moments. But I couldn't say so, didn't know how to say so.

"Max?"

And with that, I'm gone, leaving behind a room filled with memories, emotions, and a ton of unanswered questions. As I make my way through the house, my head's spinning, and the weight of what just happened starts to truly sink in.

Navigating through the throngs of people, I'm back in the heart of the party. Music still blaring, people laughing, drinks flowing—though the energy's more relaxed now, winding down. Out of the crowd, a familiar face approaches. Jake. Even though Hailey and Jake have that uncanny resemblance typical of fraternal twins, their eyes are the difference that really stands out. While Hailey's are a vivid emerald that sparkle with mischief, Jake's are a clear, striking blue.

"Hey man, where'd you disappear to?" Jake asks, clapping me on the back with a friendly thud.

"Just... upstairs," I reply, trying to sound casual.

Jake raises an eyebrow, a grin slowly forming on his face. "Upstairs, huh? Let me guess, found yourself a little company?"

I shrug, hoping to play it cool. "Maybe."

His grin widens, and he nudges me with his elbow. "Come on, spill! Who's the lucky girl?"

Trying to divert the conversation, I say, "You know me, always living in the moment. Anyway, let's not get hung up on that. Dude, we need to talk plans for the summer. We're about to have the craziest few months before college kicks off. Parties, road trips... you name it."

Jake seems all too happy to shift gears. "Hell yeah, man! This summer's going to be legendary."

As we dive into our plans, a movement on the stairs catches my eye. It's Hailey. She's descending, looking slightly disheveled. Her hair isn't as neat, her dress a bit crumpled, but damn, she's never looked more beautiful. There's an allure to her now, a post-passionate glow that makes my stomach twist in knots.

Our eyes lock for a moment, and the weight of everything that's transpired crashes down on me. There's a lot said in that look—confusion, regret, desire, and maybe a hint of anger. She swiftly diverts her gaze and continues her descent, mingling with other partygoers.

Jake, oblivious to the silent exchange, continues discussing our summer plans, but my mind is miles away. The realization hits me hard: things between Hailey and me might never be the same again.

3

Hailey

PRESENT DAY

"You've got to be kidding me."

The words tumble out of my mouth as I shut the tax ledger, shaking my head.

"Mom and Dad... this is bad."

Ten years. It's been a full decade, but as I sit in one of the cozy bedrooms of my former home—now my parents' bed and breakfast—it feels like yesterday that I was that nerdy, school-obsessed teenager. The intricate patterns of the quilt beneath me, the familiar scent of fresh linen mingling with the aroma of mom's cinnamon muffins wafting from downstairs—it's a comforting nostalgia.

Pulling out the business's books, my eyes scan the columns of numbers and notations. I might be a copyright attorney, not a tax whiz, but even I can tell that this isn't looking good. Figures don't add up, there are backlogs, and more than a few red flags that scream 'tax trouble.'

My heart sinks. Mom and Dad put their everything into this B&B, dreaming of a serene retirement as they welcomed guests and showcased the charm of Cedarwood. Now, it seems those dreams are teetering on the edge.

Exhaling a frustrated sigh, I look out the window. Cedarwood's downtown is sprawled before me, looking like a scaled-down version of Portland. There's a calmness in its quaint coffee shops, the small indie bookstore that's surprisingly resilient in the digital age, and the streets dotted with mom-and-pop stores and little boutiques. People stroll leisurely, some on bikes, and the gentle hum of life is both soothing and maddening.

How can this peaceful place be the epicenter of my current turmoil?

Ten years away, and yet, it seems Cedarwood refuses to let me go. Between memories of high school, the parties, and well... everything else, I figured this chapter of my life was sealed and stored away. But here I am, in my childhood room, trying to salvage my parents' dream.

Distractedly, I fiddle with a pencil, the tip tapping against the wooden table. The legal jargon I've grown accustomed to is vastly different from the maze of tax issues I'm now delving into. And to make matters more convoluted, Mom and Dad haven't exactly been the best when it comes to keeping their records straight. The whole thing felt like trying to untangle a huge ball of yarn.

Closing the ledger, I rub my temples, trying to stave off the headache that's been brewing. The weight of this situation feels heavy on my shoulders. But if there's one thing I've learned over the years, it's that problems don't solve themselves by brooding over them. I need a plan. Maybe an expert in town can help. Or maybe Jake knows someone from his extensive network of friends. He'd never left Cedarwood, unlike me, and had made himself something of a fixture here in town over the last decade.

Pushing back the chair, I decide to take a stroll, maybe clear my head a bit. As I head out of the room, the hallway mirror catches my reflection. Maybe it was being in my old room, but for a second, I caught sight of myself as a kid, that gawky teenager I used to be. I liked to think that young, unsure girl of ten years ago had matured into a confident woman, but right now, those eyes still reflect a hint of the kind of uncertainly they carried all those years ago.

A vibration in my pocket interrupts my thoughts. Glancing down, I see Lucy's name light up the screen of my phone. A small grin breaks my face, fond memories of our high school escapades flooding back. While I left Cedarwood, Lucy planted her roots even deeper. She's the proud owner of Mocha Memoirs, the cutest coffee-shop-slash-bookstore in town.

"Hey Hailey-bug! How's the legal eagle? Drinks later at the old Cedarwood Tavern? On me!" the text reads.

"Sounds great, Luce. Can't wait to catch up. It's been way, way too long," I reply, a warmth spreading in my chest. Lucy always had a way of making even the gloomiest days feel a tad brighter.

"Perfect! See you at 8! And wear something cute! "

I chuckle to myself. Classic Lucy. Always with a plan, always with some mischief up her sleeve.

But as I pocket my phone, the weight of the situation sinks in again. Taking a deep breath, I head downstairs to the living room. My parents, Karen and Robert, are there, waiting. Mom, with her salt-and-pepper hair neatly tied up, has those caring, blue eyes that always seem to see right through me. Dad, on the other hand, is slightly graying, a tall man who still carries himself with the air of the high school football coach he once was.

Both of them give me reassuring smiles as I enter the room. The kind of smiles that have always told me that no matter how bad things get, we're in it together.

Taking a seat across from them, I muster up all the courage I have. "Mom, Dad," I start, my voice quivering slightly, "I've gone through the B&B's books, and... well, the news isn't great."

Mom's eyes brim with concern, while Dad's brows furrow. "How bad is it?" he asks.

"We're in... significant tax debt. I don't know all the specifics yet," I confess, my stomach twisting, "but from what I can tell, if this isn't addressed soon... you could lose the business."

Silence envelops the room. I can see the fear in my parents' eyes, the realization of the dream they've built possibly crumbling to pieces. Mom takes Dad's hand, their fingers intertwining—always the united front.

"We'll figure it out, Hailey," Dad says after a long pause, determination evident in his voice. "We've weathered storms before."

Mom nods, squeezing his hand. "We'll do whatever it takes to save this place."

Dad shakes his head slightly, his eyes reflecting a mix of worry and gratitude. "And you don't need to take time off work for this, Hailey. We'll figure something out."

I cross my arms, determination setting in. "There's no chance I'm not going to help you guys. Besides, I'm such a workaholic that I've got enough PTO to take time off to build you another house with my bare hands if I need to."

Mom chuckles softly, and Dad's lips curve into a small, proud smile. "That's our girl," he says. "Always ready to take on the world."

Looking at them, seeing their unwavering spirit, fills me with a mix of pride and sorrow. "I'm going to help," I assert, "in any way I can. We're not giving up without a fight."

"Well, how bad is it?" Mom asks, her voice layered with hope and anxiety.

Rubbing the bridge of my nose, I exhale slowly. "Well, if we're talking figures... we're in the ballpark of... oh, let's say... $350,000."

Mom's eyes widen. "$350,000?! But we've been thriving! Bookings are through the roof!"

I nod, lifting a brow playfully. "Exactly. The better you do, the more Uncle Sam wants his share. It's a paradox of success."

Dad runs a hand through his hair, looking both exasperated and proud at the same time. "We kept meaning to get the taxes sorted out, you know? But between bookings, renovations, and... well, life, the years just... zipped by."

I lean back, releasing a dramatic sigh. "Trust me, I get it. Taxes are as fun as a root canal. And while I wish I had a Scrooge McDuck vault of money to bail us out, between student loans and the utterly ridiculous cost of living in Seattle, my savings are... let's just say, more along the lines of Donald Duck's."

Dad chuckles, but there's worry in his eyes. "Hailey, we can't ask you for money."

"I know," I say, "but offering is the daughterly thing to do. Besides, Jake might... oh, who am I kidding? His bar is a hit, but with his penchant for top-shelf whiskey and designer boots, I doubt he's rolling in surplus cash."

Mom looks at the both of us, her eyes twinkling despite the situation. "Well, at least one thing hasn't changed. You two still bicker like kids over who gets the last cookie."

We all share a laugh. It's short-lived, the weight of the looming debt pulling it down, but it's a reminder that together, we've weathered bigger storms.

There's a thick fog of uncertainty that hangs in the room, every one of us lost in thoughts of 'what next?'. The bed and breakfast isn't just a business; it's our family legacy, filled with memories, milestones, and a whole lot of love—not to mention that it's our home. The thought of losing it is like losing a piece of our hearts.

The room goes silent for a few moments, each of us lost in thoughts.

The plush chairs, the hardwood floors polished to a sheen, the dainty vases placed strategically around the room—this B&B is the epitome of charm. I always admired how my parents took our once chaotic, kid-ridden family home and transformed it into this boutique haven for travelers. Gone are the days of my late-night study sessions and Jake's booming music. Now, it's all about fresh linens, French toast breakfasts, and a revolving door of new faces seeking small-town serenity.

Just as I'm sinking into a comfortable nostalgia, the front door slams open with an urgency I'm all too familiar with. Jake's presence fills the room, his swagger undeniably infectious.

I've always said Jake's wardrobe looks like it was curated by someone with a hipster's heart and a GQ subscription. A snug-fitted vest over a crisp white shirt, charcoal-gray slacks, leather boots—yep, my brother's the poster child for millennial dapper. The perfectly trimmed beard and round glasses are just the cherry on top.

His blue eyes, so different from my own green ones, widen with a mix of mischief and excitement.

"You won't believe who's back in Cedarwood," he pants, his usual composure taking a backseat.

I raise an eyebrow, half-expecting him to announce the return of some indie band we obsessed over in high school. "Alright, Mr. Drama. Spit it out."

His grin is all teeth, his delight palpable. "Max Decker," he says, drawing out each syllable like it's a juicy secret.

Oh, shit.

4

Max

"Is that Max Decker?" I hear a hushed whisper. "God, he looks even better than I remember."

The familiar hum of Cedarwood's streets welcomes me as I cruise through town. There's something about the feeling of old asphalt beneath new wheels that gets the memories flooding in. My sleek black on black Ferrari 488 Spider—a far cry from the old rust bucket I used to drive back in high school—purrs as I take in the sights.

Damn, it's been a decade. Ten years since I traded Cedarwood's quiet streets for the raucous arenas of Notre Dame. A hockey scholarship there was my ticket out. From there, it was the Chicago Blackhawks, then a killer season with the Boston Bruins, and a recent trade to the Vancouver Canucks. Playing center, I have my fair share of goals, assists, and, of course, adoring fans.

But before the big-league fame and the deafening roar of NHL crowds, it was Cedarwood's icy ponds and these very streets where I skated my dreams into reality.

The downtown looks just like I remember, but a bit more... polished. Quaint shops line the street, offering everything from gourmet coffees to handmade crafts. The brickwork on the buildings seems cleaner, the windows clearer. The aroma of freshly baked bread from Millie's Bakery wafts in the air, teasing my senses.

And there it is—the spectacular coastal view at the end of the town's main street, where land meets the vast blue of the Pacific. The horizon looks like it's painted with broad strokes of oranges and purples, the sun bidding adieu for the day. That view always made me feel like Cedarwood was the edge of the world, a thought that seemed more romantic back when I was itching to leave.

Parking the car, the soft chime as I pull the keys out is drowned by a rising murmur. Seems Cedarwood hasn't forgotten its wayward son. I can feel the weight of eyes on me, some curious, some judgmental, and some undeniably female.

"Is that... is that Max?"

Straightening my jacket and running a hand through my hair, I smirk. Here we go...

"I heard he's back for some business deal," another voice speculates.

This return to Cedarwood was always going to be a trip down memory lane, but now, it's clear that lane has a cheering section.

But then, another voice pipes up, tinged with a mix of curiosity and skepticism. "What the hell is Max Decker doing back in town, especially with the hockey season on?"

A third chimes in, almost gleefully. "Haven't you heard? He's in town because he got suspended. Yeah, another publicity scandal. Seems like he can't keep himself out of trouble."

The words cut through the air, wiping the cocky smirk right off my face. I knew coming back to Cedarwood wouldn't be a quiet affair, but hearing the rumors spoken so bluntly stings more than I expected. It's a stark reminder that in this small town, news travels fast, and judgments are made even faster.

The bell above the door jingles as I slip into Mocha Memoirs, one of the new local coffee places, hoping the low brim of my hat and sunglasses will offer some anonymity. Not that I really believe it will in Cedarwood—everyone knows everyone, and they're even quicker to spot a 'celebrity' in their midst.

Mocha Memoirs is a cozy little joint, filled with the aroma of freshly ground coffee and a hint of vanilla. Exposed brick walls, mismatched chairs, and an array of plants give it a rustic charm. Fairy lights hang from wooden beams, casting a warm, inviting glow. The walls are lined with antique bookshelves packed with colorful spines. It's the kind of place that thrives in towns like this—a refuge from the hustle of big city life.

Scanning around, I spot a familiar face behind the counter: Lucy Marks. A shock of recognition runs through me. Lucy, the fierce protector of Hailey Rogers back in our high school days, and also her best friend.

From her poised stance and the way she's directing the staff, it's pretty clear she runs the show here. Damn, it's been years, but it's good to see a familiar face. I raise my hand, offering a friendly wave amidst the hustle and bustle. But instead of a pleasant acknowledgment or even a hint of recognition, she responds with a withering glare that's colder than any iced latte she's serving. Without a word or even a change in expression, she turns back to the customers, efficiently taking their orders.

Baffled, I stand there for a moment, trying to process the chilly reception. What the hell just happened? Did I step into an alternate universe where all past friendships are forgotten? Or maybe there's something I'm missing?

And sitting at a table, looking as out of place as a cat at a dog show, is my lawyer and PR-expert, Lawrence Whitfield. Tall, lean, with slicked-back silver hair and wearing a tailored suit that probably costs more than the monthly rent of this coffee shop, he's busily typing away on his latest iPhone. When our eyes meet, his thin lips twist into what I assume is his attempt at a friendly smile.

"Max!" Lawrence exclaims, standing up to greet me. He extends a hand, his grip firm. "Nice little town you've got here. Delightfully vintage. A tad too quiet for my taste, though."

I smirk, taking off my sunglasses. "Well, we can't all thrive on city smog and traffic jams, Larry."

He chuckles, though it sounds rehearsed. "True. But I have to admit, this place has its... charm. Especially if charm translates to no cell service."

"That's Cedarwood for you," I reply with a shrug.

Lawrence levels a look at me, his expression hardening. "It wasn't just 'one little incident,' and you know it. Your partying antics, the paparazzi photos with the revolving cast of women, the bar fights... need I continue? And let's not forget, these antics have gotten you suspended, in case you've forgotten."

I wince inwardly, knowing he's right, but hating to hear it. "I should be on the ice, not bumming around my hometown," I mutter.

Lawrence nods, his voice firm. "You're right. But if you want to play again, you're going to have to start by getting your reputation in order. Cementing your upcoming contract will be step one in getting you back in skates."

I let out a frustrated sigh, knowing he's right, but the reality of it all makes me feel trapped. Cedarwood, as much as I love it, was never meant to be my penance. Yet here I am, suspended from the game I love, trying to scrub clean a tarnished reputation. The road back to the ice seems longer than ever.

I lean back in my chair, blowing out a sigh. "No, you've made your point."

He nods. "We've got endorsement deals on the line, Max—especially this one with Reebok. We need to get your image cleaned up. A stint here, in this wholesome town, showing you helping out, maybe doing some charity work... It could work wonders."

I rub my temples. "So, you're telling me you dragged me back to my hometown not for a vacation, but for an image overhaul?"

"Exactly," Lawrence confirms with a nod.

I glance out the window, my eyes catching on someone familiar walking by. For a brief moment, my heart skips a beat. But she's gone before I can process it.

Refocusing on Lawrence, I reply with a smirk, "Alright, big city. Let's make Max Decker Cedarwood's golden boy again. How hard can it be?"

"I've been speaking with the reps from Reebok," Lawrence starts, eyeing me pointedly. "They're considering pulling out of the endorsement deal."

I nearly spit out my coffee. "Wait, Reebok? They're one of my biggest endorsements."

He nods grimly. "Exactly. And they don't want their brand associated with late-night bar brawls and the kind of tabloid headlines you'd find on TMZ."

I slump back, pinching the bridge of my nose. "Christ."

"And it doesn't stop there," Lawrence continues. "If Reebok pulls out, others might follow. Your team could start seeing you as a liability. Your career is on thin ice, Max."

"Got any more ice metaphors to throw at me?" I quip, though the worry is gnawing at me.

Lawrence's glare stops me cold. He's not in the mood for my brand of humor today.

Just as the weight of the situation really starts sinking in, I'm jolted from my thoughts by a timid voice. "Excuse me, Mr. Decker?"

Looking up, I'm met with the bright eyes of a kid, maybe around ten or eleven, holding up a phone. "Can I get a selfie with you? My brother won't believe I saw you here!"

Lawrence instantly scowls, opening his mouth probably to shoo the kid away, but I shoot him a warning look before turning to the youngster with a warm smile. "Of course, buddy! What's your name?"

"Tyler," he responds, his nervousness replaced by giddy excitement.

I lean in, giving the camera a cheeky grin as Tyler snaps the photo. "There you go, Ty. Now you've got proof for your brother."

"Thanks, Mr. Decker! You're the best!" Tyler exclaims with youthful enthusiasm, his eyes shining with admiration.

I can't help but chuckle, feeling a bit of a boost from the kid's awe. "Thanks, Tyler. Keep cheering, alright?"

He nods vigorously, then adds as an afterthought, "You're the best player in hockey, no matter what my dad says."

That piques my curiosity. "Oh yeah? And what does your old man say about me?" I ask, half-joking.

Tyler shrugs, his innocent face screwing up in thought. "Well, he says you're a degenerate loser who can't keep it in his pants so he can stay on the ice... whatever that means." His tone is so matter-of-fact it's clear he doesn't fully grasp what he's repeating.

My face flushes with a mix of embarrassment and irritation. "Well, tell your dad I said thanks," I reply, trying to keep the conversation light despite the sting of the comment.

Tyler nods, oblivious to the undercurrent of my words, and scampers off, probably eager to show off his prized photo.

As I watch him go, Lawrence gives me a pointed look, his expression saying loud and clear, "See what I mean?" It's a humbling reminder of how far my reputation has fallen, and just how much work I have ahead of me to turn things around. The kid's words, innocent as they are, cut deeper than I care to admit.

Lawrence just shakes his head. "Comment about your character aside, it's moments like these... Genuine interactions, that's what we need to capture and promote. Not the glitzy parties and tabloid fodder."

I lean back, sipping my coffee. "What's your point?"

Lawrence's gaze sweeps the room, settling on the various locals sipping their lattes and chatting. "These small-town people, they're grounded, sincere. If only you could find a connection here—a wholesome one. Not your usual Instagram models or those fitness influencers you always seem to attract."

I laugh, the image of settling down with a Cedarwood local playing out amusingly in my head. "So, what? You want me to waltz up to the counter and ask out the barista?"

Lawrence smirks. "If she's single and not on TikTok, then yes."

"Look," I reply, amusement evident in my voice, "I appreciate the creative PR approach, but let's not go planning my wedding just yet."

Lawrence rolls his eyes but grins. "Fine, but remember, reconnecting with your roots might just be the lifeline your career needs."

"Alright, Lawrence," I chuckle, raising my cup in a mock salute. "I'll get right on that."

"Here's your latte," a familiar voice says, as a cup is set on our table. Looking up, my heart skips a beat when I see Lucy. She's changed a bit since high school, but it's her alright.

"Ah, thank you," Lawrence says. "I took the liberty of ordering you something, Max."

"Lucy?" I manage, flashing my most charming smile.

She just raises an eyebrow, unimpressed. "Max."

I'm taken aback by the coldness in her voice. "Long time," I offer, trying to keep the mood light.

Her lips press into a thin line. "Sure has."

"Now, I can't help but notice that tone. Would I be out of line asking what it's about?" I inquire, a playful hint in my voice, though I'm genuinely curious.

Her gaze darkens for a moment, and she leans down, voice dropping so that only I can hear. "You know what you did." With that, she pivots, returning to the counter, leaving me frozen in my seat.

Lawrence, ever observant, quirks an eyebrow and takes a deliberate sip of his coffee. "Looks like you started burning bridges early. Perhaps I should've been handling your PR in high school too."

I'm momentarily speechless. Sure, I might've been a cocky kid, but what could I possibly have done to get such a chilly reception from Lucy? My mind whirls with potential scenarios, each worse than the last. The reality of returning home—complete with its ghosts and old dramas—suddenly weighs heavily on me.

As I'm contemplating this newfound mess, my phone vibrates, breaking my reverie. It's a message from Jake. 'Don't even think about skipping out. Drinks at my bar tonight. I've got stories that'll make even your hair stand on end.'

Despite the tension from the earlier interaction, a grin tugs at the corner of my mouth. Trust Jake to be the silver lining on a cloudy day. "Alright, man," I text back. "I'll be there. Prepare the strongest drink you've got."

Lawrence leans over, peering at my phone screen. "Drinks tonight?"

I nod. "Yeah, with Jake. It's been a while since we caught up."

"Just remember," Lawrence warns, pointing a finger at me, "you're here to rebuild your image. Not add to the tabloid tales."

I roll my eyes, but there's a hint of a smirk playing on my lips. "Don't worry. What's the worst that can happen? It's just a quiet drink with an old friend in a small town."

At least, I hope it is.

5

Hailey

The neon lights of the Cedarwood Tavern glow in the evening haze, offering a beacon of relaxation and, let's face it, slight inebriation. But right now, fun feels like a distant planet I'd need NASA's help to reach, with the storm brewing in the form of my family's tax crisis. Yet, there I am, wearing my 'let's pretend everything is fine' heels, lured out by Lucy's never-ending optimism.

As I draw closer, a buzz of excitement seems to hover around the entrance. Jake's place is always popular, but tonight, it's like the entire town of Cedarwood has decided it's thirsty.

And not just for drinks.

I push open the door and am immediately met with the cacophony of laughter, conversation, and music blasting from the speakers. A cursory glance around, and there it is. The source of Cedarwood's suddenly parched population. Max freaking Decker. Center of the room, holding court like a king back in his castle, surrounded by seemingly every woman in town. Figures.

Heat rises in my cheeks, partly from embarrassment over our shared past and partly because, damn him, he looks even more drool-worthy than he did a decade ago. The years have done wonders, etching a few lines of maturity onto that infuriatingly handsome face and adding an extra layer of muscle to his already impressive physique.

Ugh, why did he have to upgrade from high-school heartthrob to full-blown Greek god?

Taking a deep breath, I attempt to slink unnoticed to the bar. But let's be real—in this small town, especially in a bar this packed, unnoticed is just a fairy tale. Especially when the returning NHL star happens to be in the room.

On stage, there's a rock band giving their all, and damn, they're good. The unmistakable chords of 'Shut Up and Dance' by Walk the Moon wash over the room. A wave of nostalgia hits me so hard it's almost physical. It's like I'm right back at the school dances, surrounded by friends and, of course, drama.

The whole bar's into it now, singing along, even some brave souls dancing without a care. For a moment, despite the reason I'm here, I'm lost in the memory of those simpler times.

"Hailey!" Lucy waves me over from a corner table, a table uncomfortably close to Max and his entourage. Perfect. Just what I needed.

"Hey, Luce!" I greet her, trying to summon my brightest smile, though it probably looks more like a grimace. "Quite the crowd tonight."

I hurry over to her and it's impossible for us not to squeal with excitement. We hug hard, happiness blooming in me at the sight of my bestie.

Lucy's eyes twinkle with mischief. "Oh, hadn't you heard? Cedarwood's prodigal son has returned! And by the looks of it, he's noticed you."

My heart skips a beat as I follow her gaze. Max's stormy blue eyes lock onto mine, a hint of recognition and, dare I say, mischief flashing.

My stomach does that stupid fluttery thing, reminding me of a time when those very eyes had the power to turn my world upside down.

"Well, isn't this going to be a fun night?" I mutter, already contemplating the level of alcohol needed to navigate through this particular minefield.

Lucy, still on a roll, takes another sip from her drink and shakes her head. "He came into the shop earlier today for some meeting. Don't worry—I gave him the cold shoulder, Hales. And the coldest latte. Served him right."

"Lucy!" I hiss, my eyes darting around to ensure no one's eavesdropping. "Why would you do that? It was ages ago."

Lucy leans in, her face a picture of fierce loyalty. "He hurt you, Hailey. Badly. You might've moved on, but that doesn't mean he gets a free pass for being a grade-A jerk."

I chuckle despite myself. "A grade-A jerk who you served a grade-A cold latte? Really?"

"Well, maybe not A-grade," Lucy admits, sheepish, "More like B-minus. It was an almond milk latte, after all."

I snort into my drink, rolling my eyes. "Well, thank you for defending my honor with alternative milk. But seriously, Luce, it's water under the bridge. I mean, it's been ten years."

Lucy fixes me with a pointed look. "He broke your heart and ran off to play college puck. I remember the mess he left. You might have forgiven him, but that doesn't mean I have to. Plus, we all know what he's been up to since then."

Images of candid tabloid shots appeared in my mind totally unbidden, shots of him with whatever pop singer or model or actress had happened to catch his fancy.

"Ugh, please, not now," I sigh, feeling that weird mix of annoyance and attraction all over again.

"Fine," Lucy says with a little smirk. "But just so you know, I'm not the only one who's on to him."

As if on cue, Jake saunters over, his grin wide and inviting, a bar towel slung over his shoulder. "Hey, sis! Lucy! Having fun?"

Lucy and I exchange a glance. "Oh, a riot," Lucy deadpans. "Hailey and I were just reminiscing about high school. You remember, right? Those wonderful, carefree days full of laughter, joy, and... Max."

Jake rolls his eyes. "Oh God, you two want to talk about Decker too? Well, you're in good company with the rest of the whole damn bar here." He flashes a wry smile my way. "But if you want to reminisce about high school, how about something non-Max-related? Like... that time we toilet-papered Principal Henderson's house?"

I snicker, grateful for the change in topic. "Oh god, that was a nightmare. Remember how his dog chased us down the street?"

Jake nods, chuckling. "And how you fell right into Mrs. Thompson's rose bush? Good times."

Lucy giggles, her mood lightening. "Yeah, but let's be honest. The highlight of high school was Hailey's valedictorian speech."

I groan. "Oh, don't remind me. The projector malfunctioned, my slides were in reverse order, and I almost tripped over the mic cord."

Jake wraps an arm around my shoulder, pulling me into a hug. "But you still rocked it. Always have, always will."

Sipping my drink, I lean back in my seat, trying to process the whirlwind of faces surrounding me. Everywhere I turn, there's a former classmate, a long-lost acquaintance, a blast from my past. Well, to be accurate, Lucy's past. While she was busy racking up friends like they were going out of style, I was often found with my nose buried in a book or working on one homework assignment or another.

Jake and Lucy fall into more high school reminiscing and I take the opportunity to zone out a little bit, to try and collect myself.

The liquid courage in my glass helps dull the buzz of anxiety I feel in the crowded space. It's ironic how I managed to become a successful attorney in a big city but still feel like that awkward teenager when faced with the ghosts of high school.

My eyes drift, inevitably, to that table at the other end of the room. There, in the middle of his own adoring crowd, sits Max. Women giggle and drape themselves over him, hanging onto every word that leaves his lips. It's like a blast from the past—the high school hockey god, surrounded by his usual entourage of fawning followers. The sight would be comical if it weren't so irritating.

I take another generous sip, feeling the warmth of the alcohol spreading through me. With every passing minute and every glance in his direction, a realization bubbles up: I'm not completely over what happened. The confident, composed attorney in me wants to brush it aside, pretend it's nothing. But the teenage girl inside? The one who got her heart toyed with? She's starting to realize that, in spite of her earlier words, she's a little miffed.

Lucy, ever the observer, leans in, her eyes dancing with mischief. "You're staring," she notes playfully.

I roll my eyes, trying to play it cool. "Just observing the wildlife."

She chuckles, following my gaze. "Yeah, some things never change. Max Decker, still the king of Cedarwood."

Jake, sipping his beer, chimes in. "I mean, he's done well for himself. NHL and all."

I shrug. "So? We've all done well. Doesn't give him a free pass for being... him."

Lucy, giving me a knowing look, leans back. "There we go—not as forgiving of him as you were pretending to be, huh?"

Jake cocks his head to the side. "What're you two talking about?"

My face goes red. Jake does not know that Max was the one to take my virginity, and there's not a chance in hell I'm going to let him find out.

Lucy's eyes don't leave me, even as I take another steadying sip from my glass.

"Just how he was such a jerk to me back in high school," I said, trying to throw off the scent. "Always teasing me."

Jake laughs. "That was years ago, Hales. And he was just busting your chops, you know. Not a chance I'd ever let anyone actually pick on you. That's a big bro's job, you know?"

I laughed. "Going to take this opportunity to tell you for the ten millionth time that being born twelve minutes before me doesn't make you the older sibling."

He grins. "Sure doesn't make me the younger one, though."

I have a point, but the fact that we're fraternal twins didn't stop Jake from always looking after me like a good older brother would after his kid sister. And if I'm being honest with myself, I've always liked it.

He glances over his shoulder, spotting one of the other bartenders trying to flag him down. "Anyway, duty calls. Try to have fun tonight, OK, Hales? Hell, I bet Max would even apologize if you told him you were still pissed."

I open my mouth to make it clear that I'm most definitely not "still pissed," but Jake is already off before I get a chance. Once he's gone, I lock my eyes right onto Lucy.

My hand lands on her arm, a playful yet pointed swat. "Really, Luce?" I hiss through gritted teeth.

She just bats her lashes, innocence itself. "What?"

I level her with a look. "You know what. That was a low blow."

She leans back, regarding me with an unapologetic grin. "Come on, Hailey. It's been a decade. And if you think you can hide forever that Max Decker took your v-card, you're delusional."

My cheeks flame and I let out a groan, placing my head in my hands momentarily. "Don't remind me," I murmur, my eyes involuntarily darting towards Max, who is seated back in his throne, amidst his entourage of adoring fans.

It's a sight, alright. Max, effortlessly drawing people towards him with that magnetic charm of his. The women around him hang on to every word, offering giggles as tributes to his hockey anecdotes. And just for a second, our eyes lock. The world seems to pause, heartbeats becoming the only audible sound in the buzzing bar.

Lucy nudges me, breaking the spell. "You okay?"

I shake my head slightly, pulling myself back to the present, and throw her a tight-lipped smile. "Just peachy."

She sighs, placing a gentle hand on mine. "I'm sorry, Hales. I didn't think it would…"

I wave her apology off. "No, it's fine. It's old news. Ancient, really."

But as my eyes linger on Max a moment longer, I can't help but wonder—is it really?

And just like that, amid the mirth and nostalgia, a seed of something else takes root. A desire to confront, to clarify, and perhaps, to finally close a chapter that somehow never fully settled. The question is, am I ready to read those pages again?

It's a thought, a possibility that twinkles dimly, shrouded in layers of past pain and potent cocktails. A thought that simmers on the backburner as I refocus on Lucy, the music, and the memories that are far simpler to navigate.

But it's there, nonetheless.

As the base vibrates through the worn wooden floor, Jake sends over shots, their golden promise glinting under the lively lights. Lucy's eyes ask the question before her lips can form the words, "Are we doing this?"

I clutch the glass, a sparkle of defiance flickering through me. Screw Max, screw high school, screw it all.

"We're doing this, Luce!" One, two, three, down they go, the liquid courage tracing a warm path of daring audacity down to our bellies.

Paramore's 'Ain't It Fun' then blasts from the stage, and it's like the universe itself is daring us to defy it. Lucy grabs my hand, and we dive into the thumping, pulsing ocean of bodies, dancing our cares into oblivion.

Our moves are shameless and wild, each sway and twirl a declaration of our temporary freedom from life's sobering chains. It's Lucy and Hailey, the unbridled duo, conquering the night with every step and spin.

But even the brightest flames flicker and dim. The tune shifts into a familiar melancholy melody—'Somebody That I Used to Know' by Gotye. Instantly, it's like someone sucker-punched me right in the feels. Flashbacks flood in uninvited, memories of whispered love and promises veiled by night's comforting shadow.

I stand still for a heartbeat, lost, then shake off the shadow swiftly, morphing pain into a rhythmic sway. I won't be that girl tonight, trapped in yesterday's sorrows. Not when the night is young and the dance floor beckons with its hypnotic pulse.

Suddenly, there's a pair of hands on my hips, a physical anchor amidst the emotional whirlpool threatening to drown me.

"Hey, Hales."

I turn, locking eyes with none other than Max, whose grin still holds the power to flutter and shatter hearts in a single beat.

And there, amidst the tangled web of the past and present, the music and murmurs blending into a distant hum, we stand—locked in a moment that is as electric as it is inevitable.

6

Max

"WHAT THE HELL ARE you doing, Max?"

Hailey's words slap me out of my stupor, but damn, I can't help it. I'm looking at her, but all I see is that high school girl, amplified by a hundred, ditching the awkwardness for something fierce and smokin' hot.

I turn on the charm, grin wide, flashing my perfectly practiced, panty-dropping smile. "Hey, Hales, we've danced to this song before, remember?" There's tons of innuendo in my words, of course.

Her eyes spit fire, and man, it's not the good kind. Her fingers shove against my chest, pushing me back with a strength that's more than just physical. "Not happening, Max," she hisses, pivoting on those killer heels and darting through the crowd.

I stand there for a split second, the loud chatter of the bar fading into a distant hum as I'm left wonderstruck. The audacity! Who does that?

My brows knit together, and my feet, though momentarily rooted to the spot, decide to chase after her. But I pause, something unsettling turning in my gut. Do I really want to step into that cyclone of Hailey and all our messed-up history?

Hell, who am I kidding? Of course, I do.

I swivel toward the door, still reeling from the shock of being dismissed like I'm some second-rate player. This is me, the star center on the ice, the guy who gets any girl he wants with nothing more than a wink and a smirk.

But there's something about Hailey that flips the script. And if I'm being real, it's always been that way. At least, it had been until that one night.

Outside, I know she's simmering in a concoction of anger and whatever else that brews in the depths of those enchanting eyes. I hold my breath, the chilly metal of the door handle biting into my palm as I'm suspended between the familiar and the unknown.

A cascade of thoughts wash over me, the 'should I' and 'do I dare' doing a tango in my head.

I linger, teetering on the edge of a precipice that is the utterly mystifying Hailey. It's a junction between the comfort of my carefree, detached existence and the abyss of what-ifs that she represents.

As I stand there, a smirk tugs at my lips, an unconventional blend of confusion and exhilaration weaving through me.

I'm glued to the spot, weighing whether or not to follow Hailey into the cool night outside, a real-time war between reason and attraction playing out in my head. The noise of the bar falls away, a distant hum against the pulsating rush of blood in my ears. It's all become background noise, all the life and chatter of the bar reduced to mere spectacles in the theater of my mind, where Hailey's taken the center stage, refusing to exit.

Tiffany, one of the several girls I'd been keeping entertained earlier, a girl who'd been a freshman at high school during my senior year, slinks over. Blonde, blue-eyed, with a puck bunny vibe all over—classic Max Decker type. At any other time, I'd have basked in the attention, led her on with a grin, and a promise of a night worth her while. But not now.

"Max, what's up?" she purrs, a thin eyebrow arched in what she probably thinks is a seductive manner. "Who's that chick? She looked pissed."

I glance at her, really look at her, and for a split-second, I see every interchangeable girl I've ever been with, never a face in the crowd, never someone who could hijack my mind like Hailey just did.

Tiffany giggles, a high-pitched titter that grates on my nerves. "Wait, wasn't she that nerd from high school? What's she doing here, trying to be some kinda girlboss or something?"

My gaze hardens, the smirk fading from my face. "Watch it," I warn, my voice edged, yet composed. I may be a lot of things, but I won't let anyone sling dirt on Hailey, not when they don't know a damn thing about her.

Tiffany blinks, taken aback by the severity cloaking my words. But I've already turned away, stepping out into the night, where the sounds from the bar muffle into a distant echo.

The chill of the night grazes my skin as I spot her. Hailey, alone in the dim light, arms wrapped around herself, a fortress built of anger and vulnerability. Her eyes lift, meeting mine, a silent battlefield where neither of us holds the high ground.

It's funny. I'm Max Decker, the king of playing it cool, never letting a girl get under my skin. Yet, here I stand, rapt by a pair of piercing eyes that have always seemed to see right through me.

Something unspoken hangs heavily between us, a loaded pause in which a universe of words remains unsaid. I've never been one to back down, but confronting Hailey now feels like facing down every mistake, every wrong turn I've ever made.

It's clear she's not happy. But then again, neither am I. And maybe, just maybe, we can find a common ground in our mutual discontent, a stage upon which the next act of our intertwined tales will play out.

And in this silent standoff under the muted glow of the night, I realize that chasing after Hailey might just be the chaos I never knew I needed.

But damn, I'm going to dive in headfirst anyway.

The icy blade of Hailey's glare cuts through the chilled night, yet, undeterred, I stroll over with a nonchalance I barely feel. Her eyes, oh, those eyes, could probably melt steel with their fiery gaze, but I've never been one to back down from a challenge.

"Hey, Hales," I murmur, offering a slow, maddening grin that's usually a sure-fire winner.

"Max," she replies, her voice as cold and sharp as the autumn wind, hardly matching the heat in her eyes.

A tension coiled between us, I decide to jump right in, my curiosity piqued by the woman she's become, and my ego entirely too intrigued by her apparent disdain.

"So, Hailey... what's life been throwing at you? Still scribbling on pads, fighting the good fights with words?" I tease, keeping my tone light and my demeanor as unfazed as ever.

A thin veil of calm drapes over her as she coolly replies, "Copyright law, actually. In Seattle."

Well, color me surprised and paint me impressed. "Seattle, huh? Doing the whole 'Grey's Anatomy' rainy city love thing?"

She just arches a brow, and I can't help but chuckle at the non-answer. My hand, almost of its own volition, finds its way to her hip, brushing against the fabric of her dress. She stiffens but doesn't move away. Not yet.

I lean in closer, my voice low and suggestive, "You know, we could always slip out of here, have a more... private catch-up. Revisit some high school memories..."

The storm that's been quietly brewing in her eyes finally breaks. With a flick of her wrist, my face is drenched in the remainder of her drink, the liquid dripping down my shocked face.

"Screw you, Decker," she hisses, and with a swish of her skirt, she's gone, disappeared back into the bar from where we came.

I stand there, a cocktail of emotions stirring inside me, as the remnants of her drink slowly trickle down my skin. I'm the guy who gets every girl he wants, the eternal golden boy, at least to the public eye. I'm not used to drink-in-the-face rejections.

I wipe my face with the back of my hand, still processing the sheer ferocity in her voice, the absolute contempt in her eyes. It's unexpected, exhilarating, and to my utmost disbelief, magnetizing.

I've known plenty of women in my life, spent intimate moments with models, actresses, influencers—all of them offering gorgeous faces with smiles that never quite reached their eyes. But Hailey, she's always been real, unapologetically herself, even in her rage.

I can still remember her from high school—fierce, intelligent, and uninterested in playing the games that most girls did. And while I've been mucking around, living it up in the shallow waters of the fast life, she's turned into this... force of nature, a tempest that's just drenched me in my own smugness.

So I do what any self-respecting Max Decker would do. I laugh. Heartily, genuinely, with my head tossed back, allowing the absurdity of it all to wash over me. Because, if I'm being honest, no woman has ever thrown a drink in my face, and it's ironically refreshing.

I know I should be pissed, I know I should saunter back into that bar, find another girl to spend the night with and forget Hailey's name by morning.

But damn, if I'm not utterly fascinated by Hailey, her fire, her genuine, unbridled emotion. I'm soaked to the skin, bemused, and all I can think is that I want more.

The cool night air does little to dampen the burning curiosity that Hailey's ignited within me. So there I stand, alone in my soggy state, pondering the whirlwind that just stormed away from me.

The door creaks open, light spilling onto the concrete, and out steps Jake, a towel tossed into his hands before it finds its trajectory toward me.

"Looks like you need this, Max," Jake remarks, the hint of a teasing smile playing on his lips, despite the sternness lurking in his eyes.

I catch the towel with a half-grin, mopping at my face and shirt, "Thanks, man. Your sister sure knows how to make a statement."

Jake leans against the brick wall, folding his arms as he regards me. "I heard about what happened," he begins, "and remember, bro, my kid sister is off-limits."

I meet his eyes, the easy camaraderie we've always shared flickering with an unfamiliar tension. Truth is, I've always felt a stab of guilt about that night with Hailey back in the day, especially considering I never confessed it to Jake. He's my best friend, after all.

I shove my hands in my pockets, adopting my signature carefree grin to mask the discomfort gnawing at me. "Come on, Jake, since when do I ever go for the off-limits? I'm just having some fun."

Jake raises an eyebrow, but he doesn't press the issue. He knows me well enough to detect the nonchalance, yet chooses to let it slide, for which I'm silently grateful.

"But man, what's got her so fiery tonight?" I muse aloud, trying to shift away from dangerous territories. "She seems... I don't know, tense?"

A shadow crosses Jake's face, and he heaves a sigh, pushing himself off the wall. "Parents," he mumbles. "They're going through some serious tax trouble, could lose the house and all. Hailey's here trying to sort through the mess, help them out, and it's got her wound up tight."

A pang of sympathy jolts through me, unexpected yet potent. Hailey, with all her fierce independence, has always been fiercely protective of her family, too.

The gears in my mind begin to turn, intertwining with a crazy idea that's been fermenting in the back of my head since the tabloids got a bit too close to my personal life recently. I need a fake fiancée to get the press off my back and to inject some stability into my wild reputation. And Hailey, well, she needs money.

The dots connect seamlessly in my mind, forming a picture that's as clear as it is insane.

"And she's helping them financially too?" I inquire, trying to sound casual, yet my pulse quickens at the prospect of the gamble I'm about to take.

Jake nods, his gaze distant. "As much as she can. But lawyer or not, it's a hefty sum they're dealing with. I'm barely breaking even with this place, so not like I can help much. She's stressed, Max, so just... lay off her, alright? I know teasing is your thing, but not tonight."

I clap a hand on Jake's back, offering a comforting squeeze while a plan, dangerous and enticing, takes shape in my mind. "Don't worry, Jake. I won't ruffle any more feathers."

But as Jake heads back inside, and I'm left alone under the muted glow of the bar lights, I know that's a promise I might not be able to keep. Because if I play my cards right, I could help Hailey, help her family, and help myself.

My heart races, teetering on the brink of a decision that could either save me or plunge me deeper into a storm of my own making. And with the taste of danger on my tongue, I follow Jake back into the tumultuous sea of the reunion, my mind locked onto a path that could lead to what Hailey and I both want... or total chaos.

Sounds fun.

7

Hailey

MORNING LIGHT FILTERS THROUGH the curtains of my childhood bedroom, a subtle reminder that in Cedarwood, life moves at a deliberately slow pace. My head pounds slightly, the remnants of last night's escapades making their presence known in the form of a minor hangover. I blink, adjusting to the morning glow, and that's when I notice the little details that have always made this place home.

On the nightstand beside me, a glass of water and a couple of Tylenol tablets sit neatly, Mom's handwriting dancing on a small note beside them: "Thought you might need these, sweetheart. Love, Mom."

A small smile nudges at the corners of my mouth as I pop the tablets and gulp down the water. Mom's nurturing never ends, even when I'm now more than capable of nursing my own hangovers. The comfort of being cared for in such a tender, unspoken manner is a welcome balm against the chaos of last night.

Hauling myself up, I move towards the window, peering out at the familiar sight of Cedarwood spread out before me. Quaint houses, the charming downtown strip, and the expansive coastline shimmering in the distance—it's a postcard picture of cozy, small-town life. Cedarwood always seemed to me like a miniature Portland, teeming with life and character, yet simultaneously providing a sense of peace and escape. The trees are a riot of gorgeous fall colors, the air nice and crisp.

In the light of day, memories from mine and Max's reunion trickle back, mingling with the scent of sea salt wafting through the slightly ajar window. The dancing, the laughter, and the lightness of being with old friends—it was all a blast until a certain someone decided to make an entrance into my carefully compartmentalized memories.

Max Decker.

I shudder at the thought of his smug smile, the way his fingers brushed against my hip, and the audacity of his proposition. Could he really be so deluded, so cluelessly self-absorbed to think that his charm would have me melting at his feet?

For a moment, guilt nibbles at my conscience. Did I take it too far, throwing that drink in his face? But the answer materializes almost instantly: No. He deserved that splash of reality, maybe even needed it after years of having women throw themselves at him.

As I sit on the edge of my bed, I can't shake off the lingering tension in my muscles, the embodiment of stress and frustration that's pent up over the last few weeks. Legal jargon, tax evasion allegations, and endless paperwork clutter my mind, making the soothing embrace of a hot bath sound like a heavenly escape.

So, with a steadying breath, I pull myself towards the bathroom, deciding to indulge in a little self-care amidst the emotional minefield that's taken hold. Perhaps a good soak can wash away the icky remnants of last night, along with Max's intrusive advances.

I run the bath, the sound of rushing water a sweet symphony to my agitated senses. And as I lower myself into the steaming tub, I make a silent vow to not let Max, or anyone for that matter, steer me off course. I'm Hailey Rogers, after all, and if there's one thing I've learned in the battlefield of courtrooms and legal warfare, it's that I'm nobody's pushover.

Closing my eyes, I let the warmth seep into my pores, willing the chaos, the frustration, and Max's infuriating smirk to drown in the depths of the soothing waters.

In this tranquil solitude, I find my resolve solidifying like a rock within me. Max might have surprised me last night, but he doesn't hold any power over me. I'm in control now, and if he thinks he can play me like one of his puck bunnies, he's in for a rude awakening.

Max Decker, brace yourself. Hailey Rogers isn't a high school girl anymore. And if you think a charm offensive is going to sway me, well, I've got a few surprises of my own to unleash.

The longer I stay in the bath, however, the more I realize the water alone isn't going to take care of every need I have. My eyes drift to the tub's showerhead, the one I'd used so many times before when I needed to, ah, take care of things. Part of me wants to hop out of the tub and get on with the day. The other, however, yearns for a little recreation.

Screw it.

I grab the showerhead and here we go. Surrounded by all these suds and warmth, my mischievous mind decides to take a fun little detour. I turn on the showerhead, slipping it underneath the water and angling it between my legs, the powerful jets of water hitting me right where I want them.

"Yes... Oh, hell yes." I grin, pleasure pulsing through me as I close my eyes and focus.

It isn't long, however, before my mind starts conjuring up fantasies. And just as I don't want to happen, the fantasies are focused on one person—Max.

I groan, knowing that it's not a good idea to think about him while I'm having my special alone time. But the need is there, and it's so insistent.

Fine. What the hell? I decide that I can fantasize about him and use it to get him out of my head. Kind of like breaking the sexual tension but in a harmless sort of way. The decision made, I angle the jet again, hot delight shooting up through me as the water sprays against my clit.

His eyes pop into my mind first, always so lit with mischief and... something warmer, softer. Ugh, Max and his eyes that just seem to peer into your soul, knocking down every damn wall you've built.

And oh, that smile. That reckless, devil-may-care smile that makes you feel seen in a way you weren't prepared for. The man knows he's trouble—the fun kind.

My heart races as an imaginary Max cups my face. His thumb gently caresses my cheek, stirring something low in my belly. Gosh, even dream Max has skilled hands, I'll give him that.

Leaning in, his whispers tease my ear, honeyed words dissolving into the steam around us. A shudder of sheer delight runs down my spine, an unexpected response to this oh-so-vivid fantasy.

Now we're kissing, an easy, unhurried melding of lips that speaks of slow dances and lingering glances. His kisses are just as I remember—sweet, tempting, a promise of more.

We lose ourselves in this gentle exploration, fingers tracing familiar yet novel paths, sparking a dormant flame that seems all too willing to be rekindled.

The kiss evolves, becoming a silent communion of unspoken secrets and swallowed down confessions. And, lost in this wonderful illusion, I willingly succumb to the allure of "what if."

Then there's more. I start imagining him moving his hands between my legs, spreading my lips and slipping inside of me. We're back in his bedroom all those years ago, excitement and nervousness moving through me in equal measures. Max is on top of me, his thickness pointed right between my legs.

I place my hand on his perfect, athlete's ass and guide him down, urging him to sink into me. I gasp as he pushes inside, those stormy, blue eyes locked on mine as he moves each inch into me. It's not long before he bottoms me out. I still remember the way I felt back then, the way I'd wondered how the hell a virgin like me had been able to accommodate a cock as big as his.

Then he was moving into me, his lips moving along my neck as his manhood moved in and out, in and out. It'd been over ten years, but damned if I could remember in striking detail that perfect way he'd filled me, the sensation of him stretching me out, my walls gripping him tightly.

It didn't take much of this. The water jet angled just so, I lost myself in the trance of imagining him moving inside of me at a steady pace, each stroke bringing me closer and closer and closer until...

"Oh... Oh fuck." The orgasm rips through me and it takes all I've got to hold the showerhead in place, my body shaking from the intensity. When I'm done, I let my leg drape over the side of the tub and drop the showerhead underwater, the jets spraying against my inner thigh.

My eyes flutter open, Max's ghostly kisses still tingling on my lips. One fantasy. That's all you get.

By that point, the water was tepid. Time to go back into the real world where I was most definitely not having a fling with Max freaking Decker. I climb out and dry off, suddenly eager to get moving.

I gently push the bathroom door open, feeling a mixture of frustration and amusement at the notion of Max creeping into my headspace even in such intimate moments. Ugh, it's like high school all over again.

A towel snugly wrapped around me, I cross the space to my old bedroom, images of Max's smirking face refusing to leave my mental view. How annoyingly perfect must a man be to persistently intrude upon my thoughts like that insufferably catchy pop song he'd taken my virginity to?

Dressing in a casual tee and jeans, I catch sight of my reflection in the mirror. "New day, new mindset, Hailey," I tell myself, putting on a determined look, trying to muster the spirits of all the badass women in pop culture to assist me in exorcising this Max Decker ghost from my psyche.

Slipping into a pair of denim jeans, I try to push away the rising tide of memories threatening to drown my senses in a sea of frustration and desire. The simple act of dressing, of feeling fabric slide against skin, becomes a cruel reminder of hands that weren't mine exploring uncharted territories with fearless abandon.

My hands momentarily freeze on the zip, my mind betraying me with flashes of Max's lips, skilled and insistent, mapping a path down my neck, as his hands, strong yet gentle, deftly moved with a familiarity that belied our age. His body, a sculpture of lean muscles and sun-kissed skin, had looked like a piece of art under the dim lighting of his bedroom that fateful night, the memory vivid even after all these years.

With a muffled scream into the abyss of my empty room, anger surges through me, directed inward for allowing those memories to retain their potency, and outward at Max, for strolling back into my life as if he owns every piece of it, re-igniting a fire I thought had long been extinguished. As I pull a sweater over my head, I vow to myself that Max Decker will not have the satisfaction of seeing me unravel.

My reflections stare back at me, a myriad of emotions flickering in my eyes. With a steadying breath, I solidify my resolve, armoring myself against the enigmatic power he seems to wield over me. But even as I mentally construct these fortifications, part of me wonders whether they will be enough against the impending storm that is Max Decker.

As I make my way downstairs, the cheerful sound of conversation and laughter wafts toward me. I anticipate the presence of my parents and Jake, perhaps reminiscing over old times. The homey scent of coffee fills my nostrils. It's comforting, a reminder of the serene and loving atmosphere I grew up in.

But as I step into the doorway of the dining room, my heart falls into my stomach. There, amid the cozy scene of my family enjoying breakfast, sits Max Decker, his tall frame relaxed in the chair, a charming smile spread across his face as he animatedly talks to my mom.

She's laughing heartily at whatever tale he's spinning, apparently completely charmed by him. Jake gives me a wink as I enter, seemingly oblivious to the awkward confrontation from last night. My dad looks up and offers me a warm, albeit somewhat tired smile.

"And look who's finally up!" My mom exclaims, her eyes lighting up at my entrance. "Hailey, we have a guest for breakfast."

My eyes flicker to Max, who's now sporting a smirk that is so quintessentially him, the one that screams mischief and boyish charm. It takes all the strength in me not to show my disturbance at his unexpected presence.

I muster the brightest, most unaffected smile I can. "I see that. Good morning, Max."

"Morning, Hales." His voice is buttery, almost flirtatious, and the familiar nickname sends a tiny, involuntary shiver through me.

Suppressing a grimace, I find a seat as far away from him as the table permits, then serve myself a generous portion of scrambled eggs and hash browns, focusing on the food rather than the unwanted guest.

"Max was just telling us about his travels during the off-seasons," my mom shares excitedly. "Did you know he went skydiving in New Zealand?"

"Oh, it's nothing compared to the thrill of seeing Hailey again," Max interjects smoothly, his eyes dancing with unspoken amusement as they lock with mine.

I nearly choke on my coffee. "Is that so?"

"Absolutely. Cedarwood is always full of surprises."

8

Max

"MAX, YOU ARE TOO much," Hailey's mom speaks the words with total warmth.

"Yeah," Hailey adds. "I'll say." These words, on the other hand, are as cold as a hockey rink on gameday.

A smirk plays on my lips, unbridled and daring, as I lounge in Hailey's parents' cozy dining room. A steaming mug of the strongest coffee I've ever had is cradled between my hands, and the rich aroma intermingles with the scent of fresh waffles wafting through the air. The picture of homely serenity is almost convincing enough to eclipse the razor-sharp glares Hailey is shooting my way from across the table. But damn, even her irritation is luminous, casting an unexpected thrill down my spine.

Oh, this is great, I think, casually leaning back in the worn but comfortable chair, basking in the unnervingly tranquil environment of the Rogers family breakfast tableau. A paradox, considering the turbulent storm brewing just a few feet away in the form of a petite, auburn-haired tempest named Hailey. She's fuming, but her silence is golden, at least for now.

"So, Mr. and Mrs. Rogers," I say, laying on my most charming, boy-next-door grin. "I was hoping to steal Hailey away for a little chat, if that's alright with you." My eyes flick to hers, a challenging spark igniting in the depths of my gaze.

Her parents, sweet and unsuspecting, exchange a glance, that knowing, parental look that teases of matchmaking and nostalgia for youthful romance. "Of course, Max," Mrs. Rogers responds with a tender smile, her eyes twinkling with mischief and gentle encouragement.

Mr. Rogers, a mirror image of an older, distinguished Jake, nods in agreement, his demeanor gentle yet guarded, protective instincts barely concealed beneath a surface of warm hospitality. "Just remember," he begins, his voice steady and amiable, "that's our little girl." He chuckles, letting me know he's only giving me the business.

"Always, sir," I reply with practiced sincerity, offering a reassuring nod. "I've only got the utmost respect for Hailey." And that's no lie, respect is there, amongst a tangle of other, more convoluted emotions.

With an inward chuckle, I stand, extending a hand to Hailey with a flourish, eyebrow raised in a silent dare. She looks at it as though it's a venomous snake, her eyes ablaze with unspoken words, but I see it—a flicker of curiosity beneath the inferno.

The seed is sown, the players set, and the game? Oh, it's most definitely on. Now, all that's left is to draw Hailey into my plot, into a web weaved of desperation and necessity. But as she places her hand reluctantly in mine, I'm struck by a pang of something unidentifiable, a subtle, unsettling squirm in my gut, and I'm left wondering if Hailey Rogers might just be the spider in this particular web, rather than the fly.

The moment Jake and his parents depart from the scene, the atmosphere tangibly shifts, Hailey's furious eyes locked onto mine, questions, and undoubtedly a cascade of scathing remarks, hanging in the tension between us. But she surprises me, holding herself with a restrained, quiet anger. A controlled storm.

"Max," she begins, her voice cool and steely, "You've got exactly thirty seconds to explain why the hell you're sitting in my parents' dining room before I throw you out myself."

My shoulders roll back, a deliberate exhale passing through my lips as I prepare myself to dive into this tempest. "First things first, Hales. I owe you an apology for last night," I admit, catching her off-guard with a sincerity she probably didn't expect from me. "I was out of line and, hell, downright disrespectful. I'm sorry."

A flicker of surprise crosses her expressive eyes, and her stance softens just a touch. But it's not enough, and I know I've still got mountains to climb.

Her voice is softer, simmered, but still steady when she speaks. "Is that all you think you should be apologizing for, Max?"

My brows knit together, genuine confusion furrowing my forehead as I meet her pointed gaze. Was there more? My mind momentarily darts back through our past interactions, scouring for a misstep I might have missed. "I wasn't aware there was something else I needed to apologize for," I reply cautiously, letting a playful, challenging grin tease at the corner of my mouth, "with you, at least."

The faintest quirk of her lips suggests she's not entirely immune to my charm, but she remains composed, a guarded sentinel of emotions. With a controlled inhale, Hailey crosses her arms, her curiosity now fighting with her ire.

"Alright, Decker. You've piqued my interest. Spill. What's this really about?"

Another pause, another heartbeat, and then I dive into the abyss of my audacious scheme. "I've got a proposal for you, Hailey. A wild, batshit crazy proposal," I lean forward, locking eyes with her, the spark of an adventurous challenge lighting up my expression. "But it's one that could seriously work out for both of us... if you hear me out."

A pregnant pause hangs in the air between us, the words of my implication suspended like a tightrope I've just invited her to walk upon.

"A proposal?" Her voice carries a note of incredulity mixed with an undeniably potent dash of intrigue.

I lean back, my confident, cocky demeanor securely back in place as I nod. "Yep. And when I say 'proposal,' I mean that in the most literal sense, Hales."

Her eyes flicker, a tumult of thoughts and emotions dancing in those emerald depths, and I can't help but be drawn into the mystery of Hailey Rogers, wondering if this venture might be more complex than I'd anticipated.

My heart's pulsing in a frenetic beat, a peculiar mix of anticipation and apprehension mingling as I hold Hailey's gaze, gauging her reactions with an acute, sharp attentiveness. There's a lot hanging in the balance here, and I can sense the precariousness of the thread by which this whole mad plan dangles.

I tilt my head slightly, an amused smirk drawing on my features as I kick-start this lunatic pitch. "So Hailey, do you know why I'm gracelessly disrupting the peace of Cedarwood, to begin with?" I venture, lifting an eyebrow, injecting a lightness into the heavy atmosphere between us.

She snorts, the unmistakable fire of her character blazing through her restrained demeanor. "Let me guess, Max, another romantic entanglement gone awry?" Her voice is drenched in a potent mix of disdain and genuine curiosity. "I'm not exactly president of your fan club, so my knowledge is a bit limited in the scandalous life of Max Decker."

I can't help it; I chuckle, entirely disarmed by the sassy allure of her wit. "You always did have a knack for cutting through the bull, didn't you, Hales?" I admit, leaning back slightly, the charisma I've always wielded like a weapon, now dipped in a genuine respect for her moxie.

"You're not entirely wrong. Got caught in a bit of a stormy love triangle. Picture this: a high-profile model, Katrina Velasquez, on one arm and pop sensation Lyla Simms, known for her not-so-subtle ballads about ex-lovers, on the other. I bet you can imagine how well that unfolded in the public eye."

Her eyes dance with a mix of amusement and disbelief, clearly finding some petty joy in my misadventures.

"The blowback," I continue, "hit harder than expected. Fans, especially Lyla's—who are, let's say, devoutly intense—are out for my blood. Sponsors are second-guessing their associations. Poor Max Decker, the golden boy of the NHL, is now public enemy number one in the romantic realm."

She raises an eyebrow, a smirk playing on her lips, "And why, pray tell, is your latest romantic debacle of any concern to Hailey Rogers?"

"Oh, it isn't," I retort quickly, my gaze flicking pointedly around the room, "Your problem is a bit closer to home, isn't it?" I pause for impact, letting the implication of the house, of her parents, hang heavily in the air between us.

Hailey says nothing, her eyes betraying the flicker of vulnerability that she's trying so hard to mask. She's silent, but I can see the wall she's built wavering, just slightly, under the weight of familial obligations and financial burdens.

"So here's where the madness comes into play," I lean in slightly, my voice a conspiratorial whisper, feeling the adrenaline course through me as I dare to lay out the unhinged strategy that had formulated in my reckless brain.

"You and I, Hailey, get married."

9

Hailey

FALL IN CEDARWOOD IS like a living, breathing postcard—it's all warmly-hued foliage softly rustling in the gentle breeze, snug little cafes emitting the comforting aromas of pumpkin and cinnamon, and cobblestone streets dotted with locals wrapped in cozy knits, their breath visible in the crisp, chilled air.

It's the kind of place where charm is not merely an attribute but an intrinsic quality, woven into the very fabric of the town. And right now, that idyllic tranquility clashes hilariously with the utter absurdity unfolding in my current conversation.

I'd needed a moment, some fresh air after Max had made his little oh-so-literal proposal.

Max and I walk side by side, yet in disparate worlds. My mind is a veritable tornado of disbelief, confusion, and oddly, a sliver of consideration. His proposition is ludicrous, isn't it? And yet, as we stroll through the golden-canopied streets, under the watchful gaze of the quaint, slightly weathered shopfronts of Cedarwood, I can't bring myself to outright dismiss the thought.

As much as I want to lean into the anger bubbling within me, there's this pesky, rational part of my brain, considering the feasibility, probing the possibility, despite how much I want to slap that smug grin right off his infuriatingly handsome face.

"I..." My voice teeters on the brink of stability and I take a moment, steadying my breath, gazing at the beautiful pandemonium of colors adorning the trees above us, "What are you even talking about, Max?" I finally manage, my voice a quiet yet potent mix of defiance and curiosity. "Explain everything."

He doesn't break stride, his hands tucked casually into his pockets, his eyes reflecting the vivid autumnal shades overhead. "It's simple," he offers, his tone frustratingly nonchalant, "You and I get married. Like I said."

I stop in my tracks, my boots clicking sharply against the cobblestones, and turn to face him, my gaze narrowed and brow furrowed in exasperation. "That, Max," I retort, a brittle laugh escaping my lips, "is about the least simple thing I can imagine."

He concedes with a nod, his eyes meeting mine with a strange sincerity that disarms me, just a fraction. "Fair point," he admits, the subtlest hint of vulnerability flickering through his otherwise composed demeanor.

The quaint, whimsical charm of Cedarwood wraps around us, a stark contrast to the absurdity weaving through our discourse. My arms instinctively cross over my chest, a barrier as I mutter, the words just barely audible, "Then tell me."

And as he steps closer, the distance between us a mere whisper, I find myself caught between the desire to flee and the inexplicable urge to leap into this maelstrom of madness, if only to see where it might lead.

"I'm not trying to play the victim here, Hailey," he admits, eyes shadowed with a rare introspection that is as captivating as it is disconcerting. "I've made a mess of things, and yeah, I've earned every shred of this bad reputation."

I arch a brow at his unexpected self-awareness. "Glad to hear there's at least a morsel of humility in there, Decker," I retort, my voice laced with a sass that conceals an unwilling intrigue in the outlandish plot he proposes.

My boots click rhythmically against the pavement, a melodic counterpoint to the chaotic thoughts swirling through my mind as we reach Cedarwood's charming downtown. It's a picturesque tapestry of rustic boutiques, cozy coffee shops with patrons nestled in corners, engrossed in conversations or books, and ornate street lamps poised like silent sentinels over the bustling town center. Crimson and amber leaves flutter gently down from the trees lining the streets, settling on cobblestone paths and charming storefronts.

He pauses, looking around at the tranquil scene, perhaps seeking solace in its undisturbed beauty amidst his own storm.

"I know it's... crazy," he concedes softly, "But this plan, it's not just a game to me. I'm screwed, Hailey. If I don't turn things around, my career, everything I've worked for—it's all on thin ice."

His use of a sports pun doesn't escape me and despite the gravity of the situation, a sardonic smirk plays upon my lips. "Max, I'm not your savior. I'm not some fixer-upper fairy godmother who can just wave a wand and clean up your mess," I reply, though my voice is devoid of the harshness I'd intended.

I glance around, suddenly keenly aware of the subtle yet unmistakable glances cast our way, the surreptitious nudges and whispers exchanged amongst locals, as they steal not-so-covert looks at Max—and by proximity, me.

He catches one of the glances, returning it with a practiced, nonchalant smile before turning back to me, eyes aflame with a sincerity that tugs, unexpectedly, at my resolve.

"I know that, Hailey," he answers quietly, "And I'm not asking you to be. All I'm asking is for a chance to prove that beneath all the screw-ups and the reputation, I can be someone worth standing beside. Even if it's just pretend."

It's an allure wrapped in potential catastrophe, his eyes pleading silently for a chance I'm not sure I'm brave—or foolish—enough to give. My heart wavers, caught between the echoes of past heartbreak and the precipice of an unforeseen adventure, as I stand, suspended, on the brink of a decision that could either save us both or drag us under.

"Alright, Max," I say, a strange concoction of dread and excitement bubbling within me, "Spin me the whole yarn. Let's hear how you've scripted our grand love story."

Max's eyes light up, a sparkle of mischief dancing in them as he leans in, lowering his voice to a conspiratorial whisper. Even though we're pretty much alone on this charmingly vacant street, draped in autumn colors, he's got that dramatic flair that demands indulgence.

"Alright, Hailey. Picture this," he begins, hands gesturing elaborately, crafting the narrative in the air between us. "A reunion of two former high school loves."

"We were hardly—"

"I know, I know. But bear with me—creative license and all that."

I let out a dry laugh. "Fine. Go ahead."

"I'm back in my hometown on sabbatical, and you're here to help out your family. And one night, we lock eyes across the crowded bar, and it's like no time has passed at all."

I tilt my head, arms crossed, decidedly unimpressed but silently egging him on with a raised eyebrow.

He continues, unabashed, "The tabloids will eat it up, right? Two old flames, reigniting amidst the flicker of fairy lights and to the nostalgic strains of whatever one-hit-wonders we danced to back in the day."

"Fairy lights?" I interject with an amused smirk, but he waves me off, spiraling further into his constructed reality. "Jake's bar isn't exactly the fairy light sort of joint."

"Yes, absolutely essential for the aesthetic, trust me," Max insists, an impish grin forming. "Anyway, there we are, laughing, dancing, all those lost years melting away in an instant."

I roll my eyes but let him continue. The absurdity of it all is somehow entertaining, a welcomed diversion from the heavy weight of reality, and I'm curious about how far his imagination stretches.

He takes a dramatic pause, "The night ends, we promise to keep in touch this time, but then, oh no—I have to leave soon, back to the life of an NHL star."

"Oh, the tragedy," I murmur, feigning desolation, and he flicks a playful glare my way before plunging back into his tale.

"But then! I can't stop thinking about you," he says, taking a step closer, his voice softened, attempting sincerity and failing spectacularly. "Life suddenly feels empty because you're not there."

I can't stifle the laugh that bubbles up, "Max, you should've been an actor with this level of drama."

He ignores my jab, theatrically placing a hand over his heart, "Heartbroken, I realize what I must do. I need to chase after what's been missing all these years."

I chortle again, shaking my head. "You're laying it on thick even for a tabloid love story."

With a sly, confident grin, Max shrugs, "Go big or go home, right? Next thing you know, I'm on your doorstep, no cameras, no entourage, just Max Decker, humbled by love."

"You? Humbled?" I scoff, but the spark of amusement in my eyes betrays my enjoyment of his ludicrous romantic tale.

"And then," he leans in, his voice a hushed whisper, as if sharing a coveted secret, "the bad boy of the NHL proposes, not caring for a moment about the prying eyes of the media or the whispers of the past, only seeing the woman who's managed to capture his wayward heart."

He steps back, spreading his arms wide, "End scene."

I blink at him for a moment, a laugh perched on the precipice of my lips. Despite the ridiculousness of it all, there's something undeniably fun about this imagined spectacle, a wild departure from the dreariness of looming debts and desperation.

With a dramatic bow, Max seeks approval, "So, Hailey, what do you think of our enchanting love story, destined to captivate the masses?"

"Let me get this straight," I begin, my voice is airy, carrying an intentional frivolity to hide the storm of thoughts inside. "You want me, the 'wholesome girl-next-door,' to be the fake fiancée of the 'reformed' bad boy, just to clean up your tarnished image?"

He simply nods, his grin holding steady. "Exactly, you've got it. I mean, who wouldn't believe it? The notorious player finally tamed by the one that got away, it's pure gold."

I snort, unable to contain the outburst. The sheer audacity of it all. "You're delusional, Max."

He starts walking, and I find my feet moving to keep pace. There's a bounce to his step, a lightness that clashes harshly against the gravity of his proposed sham.

"And after a suitable amount of time, we just... end it? No harm, no foul, we just say 'whoops, better as friends' and that's that?" I ask, incredulity lacing my voice, all while imagining the headlines, the gossip articles, the paparazzi...

"Precisely. But all friendly and mutual. It's like... we're doing each other solid favors. I have a mature engagement, and then a mature breakup—no hard feelings. Then, when it's all said and done, I get my image rehab and you..." he trails off, turning to me with that signature, cocky Max Decker charm.

I cut him off before he can finish, "Save my family's house from being a hipster coffee shop's new location?"

"Bingo."

I consider his words, my mind whirring a mile a minute as I weigh up the pros and cons. The logical part of me is screaming to throw his proposal into the harbor and run for the hills. Yet, there's this reckless, daring part that's intrigued by the madness of it all.

"You're saying you'd pay off all of our debts?" My voice lowers, becoming a mere whisper, a stark contrast to the casual tone from a moment ago. "You realize that's not chump change, right?"

He stops and pivots towards me, his expression shifting from play-ful to intensely serious. "Every penny, Hailey. I've done well for myself, not to brag. But if I can hang onto these sponsorships, sign a few new contracts, I'll be one of the highest-paid athletes in history."

My thoughts race, images of my family being evicted flashing through my mind, mingled with the potential headlines chronicling my inevitable, public faux-romance with Max. As I glance up, meeting his earnest gaze, the decision teeters dangerously on the edge of my tongue.

Max's hands gently encasing mine shift the atmosphere entire-ly, causing an unexpected flutter in my chest. His eyes search mine, searching for an answer that I'm not quite ready to give.

"Take your time, Hailey," he murmurs, the gruffness of his voice nearly masked by its tenderness. "Think it over. I'll be at the Cedar-wood Grand in the Presidential Suite. When you're ready... you know where to find me."

A small sigh of relief escapes me as the pressure lifts momentarily, offering a brief reprieve from the chaos this day has thrust upon me. Before I can fully settle into that comfort, Max's voice lowers to an almost seductive whisper.

"But," he starts, a devilish grin tugging at the corner of his lips, "let's leave them with a little something to talk about, shall we?"

The bemusement barely has time to cross my face before his lips are on mine, strong, insistent, and undeniably skilled. In front of the entire town. In the center of the cozy, tree-lined street. Max Decker is kissing me as though he's got every right to, a possessive yet passionately exploratory kiss that, despite my better judgment, I find myself reciprocating.

And then, as abruptly as it began, he pulls away, his forehead resting against mine, allowing us both to catch our breaths. His eyes, unreadable, lock with mine, and for a moment, we're suspended in this crazed reality he's proposed.

Then, just as quickly, he's pulling back, that cocky, charming smile firmly back in place as he gives my hand one last reassuring squeeze, and then he's gone, disappearing into the maze of Cedarwood's quaint downtown.

"Hoping for good news," he tosses over his shoulder before turning around the next corner and vanishing.

I'm left standing there, my hand absently rising to touch my still-tingling lips, the whispers and stares of the townspeople encircling me like a curious mist. They've got their spectacle, and I've got a monumental decision to make.

10

Max

I'M STAYING AT THE Cedarwood Grand, a beacon of luxury amidst the quaint surroundings of Cedarwood. Built in the past half-decade, it's easy to see how it caters to the new wave of high-end tourists drawn here by the town's viral social media presence. Sleek glass facades reflect the surrounding natural beauty, and the modern aesthetic contrasts with Cedarwood's rustic charm.

The ambiance screams 'trendy luxury,' from the chic furniture to the intricate art pieces dotting the walls. It's a fusion of the old and the new, and I can't help but be impressed. This place is worlds apart from the Cedarwood I once knew.

And it's among this hip ambiance in my penthouse suite where my phone blares, ripping through the muted hum of the space.

"Well, what happened?" the voice on the other end doesn't wait for formalities, in typical Lawrence fashion.

My brows knit together, the trace of annoyance seeping into my tone. "And hello to you too, oh agent of mine."

"Don't play cool, Decker," he spits out, an audible exhale of impatience rustling through the line. "Did you get the girl on board or what?"

I lean back, the worn leather of the armchair creaking beneath me, my eyes tracing the mundane patterns of the hotel wallpaper. "She's mulling it over. I'll have an answer by tonight," I respond, a casualness in my voice that only slightly masks the underlying tension.

"Good enough, I suppose." A pause, and then Lawrence's voice dips, lacing his next words with a sinister smoothness. "Look, once she agrees, play the doting fiancé for a few months, and then you can dump her and this Hicksville. You won't have to deal with them ever again."

My jaw clenches, a surge of unexpected protectiveness welling up inside me. This isn't just any girl he's talking about—it's Hailey. And Cedarwood isn't just any town. "Watch it, Larry," I snap, my words sharp and edged. "That's a childhood friend and my hometown you're running down."

A long, languid sigh filters through, and I can almost picture Lawrence rolling his eyes. "Fine, fine," he says, but the condescension clings to every syllable. "Just make sure you wrap this up quickly, alright? The longer this drags on, the higher the risk it all falls apart."

His words hang in the air long after the call ends, an omen darkening the mood of the dimly lit room. My eyes drift to the window, beyond which lies the town that shaped me, and the girl who's inexplicably wormed her way back into my thoughts.

Lawrence doesn't get it. To him, people and places are pawns, easily discarded when their purpose is served. But despite the charisma, the parties, the carefree persona I've crafted so meticulously... I'm not him.

As the thought of Hailey lingers in my mind, creating a complex tapestry of 'what ifs' and possibilities, I'm left wondering if this fake love story could somehow reroute my twisted path.

One thing's for damn sure—I need a workout. Nothing helps work through stress like hitting the weights hard, and I'm desperate for anything to take my mind off Hailey and the insane proposal I'd thrown at her. After changing into some workout clothes, I head down to the hotel's gym and get to work.

***

Burning through my workout, my muscles stretch and pull, but it's Hailey stretching through my mind that's really throwing me. That bookish, understated girl from high school, with a quiet sort of hotness she seemed clueless about.

Man, how she's shifted gears from then to now, even with those librarian vibes, she's become a stunning, sassy woman. I can practically hear the laughter, see that carefree, dancing spirit from the bar, and it's messing with my focus big time.

Lifting weights should shove aside these nagging thoughts, but it's like she's stuck to me. My mind keeps replaying our last encounter, her eyes, a mix of shock and something deeper, as I kissed her. It was meant to be a part, a role in this wild plot, but the feel of her lips, that faint, sweet taste, it's stuck with me, blurring lines that should have stayed sharp.

Even here, in my usual escape hatch of a workout, she's tangled up in every thought, no answers, just more damn questions.

A glance at the TV throws me off again. My face is plastered on the screen, "Max Decker's Love Life Disaster" glaring below snapshots of me down in LA, doing... all the stuff I liked to do down there. Seriously? I snap it off, hating how even this space is now invaded by that incessant, public hum.

Dropping the weights, my reflection stares back, muscles and all, but there's a vulnerability in the eyes looking back at me. Something unfamiliar and way off-script.

Hailey. Meant to be the neat answer to a PR nightmare, and instead, she's under my skin, working her way deeper and deeper.

My usually shielded heart is dangling on the edge, exposed and to be honest, I'm not so sure I can, or want to, pull it back to safety. And that, that right there, is a whole new game, isn't it?

When I'm done, I head back to my room and strip down, ready to hit the showers and wash away the traces of the workout—and hopefully to rinse Hailey out of my thoughts.

Sizzling water pelts down on me, steam swirling and mingling with the cascading droplets. Hailey. That name. It's looping in my head, an unbroken reel of those sun-kissed freckles, and that sass that makes you want to kiss her and argue with her at the same time. A shiver runs through me, and not from the cooling water.

I let memories play—her laughing eyes, the gentle sway of her dance at the bar, her voice that speaks eloquently even when she's chucking sarcastic bombs. With a certain reluctance, I try to shove her face to the back of my mind, focusing instead on the tiles of the shower wall.

Alright, now shower time's supposed to be Max Time, you know? A moment to wash away all the day's worries, sweat, and to just have a moment with me, myself, and I. But man, the second that hot water hits me, my thoughts are doing this rebel thing where they cartwheel straight into a Hailey-fantasy-land.

There she is, that ridiculously beautiful woman with the eyes that seem to light up galaxies, standing just a bit too close, looking up at me with this impish grin. Her voice, even in my imaginings, is this soft, melodic hum that sends shivers racing down my spine.

"Max," she says, that cheeky grin transforming into a sly smirk that tells me she's up to no good... and I'm all in for it. "Tell me... tell me what you want."

Fuck. Back in the real world, I know there's no point in denying what I want. I open my eyes and glance down, and sure enough, I'm hard as a hockey puck down there, my cock pointed straight again. With a grin, I reach down and wrap my hand around my length, stroking slowly as I close my eyes and go back to the fantasy.

I pull her close, her head nestling comfortably in the crook of my neck. And there it is, that damn intoxicating scent of hers, whispering secrets and unspoken wishes into my ear, nudging at memories I've tried—and clearly failed—to stow away.

Our eyes lock, and there's that flicker, that electricity that's always buzzed between us, dormant yet undeniably present.

We're leaning into a kiss—slow, so damn slow that it's torture, but the sweetest kind, you know? Her lips brush against mine, a whisper of a touch, yet enough to send my senses into a tailspin.

The kiss deepens, a gentle exploration of remembered passion and unchartered territories. It's sweet and slow, a promise wrapped in every lingering caress, every stolen breath.

I reach down, putting my hand between her legs and feeling her warmth on my skin. I move up, up, squeezing the soft skin of her inner thigh and focusing on her breath on my neck. It's been *years* since we slept together, but all the details are so fresh, easier to remember than any of the many, many women I'd been with over the years.

I touch her, spread her lips open and watch as her eyes close and her mouth parts. I tease her clit, making slow circles until I bring her to orgasm, my hand on the small of her back as she comes.

"More," she says. "I need more."

More is exactly what I want to give her. I kiss her hard again, her tongue dancing with mine, her taste washing over me for just a moment before I grab her by the hips and turn her around. Hailey's ass is *eternally* burned into my mind, that perfect, round little thing. I grab onto her hips and pull her onto my cock, a gasp pulling into her lungs and her back arching as I fill her.

That's it, right there—that's the fantasy I'm going to finish to. Back in the real world, I'm stroking like a madman, imagining her tight walls doing the work my hand is. I focus on the fantasy, picturing her ass bouncing off of me again and again as I reach around and take hold of her swaying tits.

"Just like that, Max, just like... *ah!*'

She grips me tightly as she comes, her walls clenching around my thickness. I come with her, focusing on the sensation of shooting my seed deep inside, giving her every last drop I've got.

And when the pleasure fades, so goes the fantasy. I'm back in the shower all by my lonesome, not a Hailey in sight.

That's the one you get, Decker. I'm sure I don't even need to explain why it's a bad idea to fantasize about that one.

All the same, the memory taunts me: that lone night years ago, the small part of our past that never faded, always lingering somewhere in the corridors of my thoughts. How the hell does she still manage to seem so vivid, so tantalizing, when so much time has passed?

I wash off the evidence of my fantasy and finish up in the shower.

Toweling off, I'm caught in a reflection. Not in the mirror, but in my own conscience. Hailey isn't some media prop; she's real, flesh and blood, with dreams and disappointments. My plan—no matter how mutually beneficial I want to spin it as—drags her into a spotlight she never sought. Sure, it solves my PR catastrophe, but at what cost to her?

Would she actually say yes? She's savvy, smart enough not to get swayed by a few honeyed words and a practiced smile. And yet, that spark, that tiny glimmer when our eyes locked during that stolen kiss on the street—it told a story. An unwritten, unsettled story.

I think back to the pseudo-scenario I had painted for her, the picture-perfect love story we'd sell to the world. Me, the redeemed bad boy coming back to his roots, and her, the unspoiled hometown girl who always held my heart. We'd be the media's darling redemption and romance story rolled into one. It's so beautifully scripted, yet so incredibly fraudulent.

Grabbing my phone, I flick through social media and, sure enough, our little public display of affection has made some headlines. There's a mixture of public awe and skepticism, two components that sum up my own feelings pretty accurately.

Even with a solution to my career woes potentially within grasp, I can't shake a burgeoning dread: that I'm entangling someone I care about in a web of high-stakes deceit.

As I slump onto the edge of the bed, I'm grappling with this whole insane proposition, the conflicts are loud and clanging in my head. It's not just her decision that's hanging in the balance; it's my integrity too.

It's going to be a long wait until tonight.

11

Hailey

"He WHAT?" The words explode from Lucy's mouth like a firework, causing a few patrons at the coffee shop to give me quizzical, slightly annoyed looks.

Lucy's eyes widen, her hair bobbing as she shifts in her chair, and she grabs my arm, "Hales, please tell me you're joking. He proposed a fake engagement?!"

I nod, raking my fingers through my hair, processing everything once again. "He did. And you know the craziest part? I'm actually considering it!"

Lucy's eyebrows shoot up, a knowing smirk on her lips. "Well, it's Max. Mr. Tall, Dark, and 'I'm Too Handsome for My Good.' But seriously, it sounds bonkers."

"I know! But..."

"But?"

I sigh, the weight of the decision pressing down on me. "It could be the miracle we need, Luce. One hefty paycheck and we could save the house."

Lucy purses her lips, deep in thought. "There's also another thing..."

I squint at her, already dreading the addition to our conversation. "What?"

She leans forward conspiratorially, "This could be your golden ticket to finally make Max apologize for ghosting you back in high school. You know, a little poetic justice?"

My nose wrinkles, pushing the memory to the background. "Lucy, I'm over it. It's Mom and Dad I'm worried about."

Lucy gives me a pointed look. "You might be over it, but don't you want him to squirm just a bit? I mean, it's a win-win. He pays up, you get your apology, and maybe a little fun teasing Mr. NHL Superstar along the way."

I snort, the image of Max Decker, the pride of the NHL, squirming under my thumb is amusing. But then the sheer weight of it all crashes down again. "This isn't a rom-com, Luce. This is my life. Our family's life."

Before Lucy can offer another consoling or teasing comment, she glances at the counter, her eyes lingering at the growing line and her staff running around behind the counter. "Break's over," she mouths.

With a resigned sigh, Lucy stands, brushing invisible dust off her apron. "Just think it over, Hales. Whatever you decide, we've got your back."

I nod, trying to force a smile. "Thanks, Luce. I'll... I'll think about it."

She gives my arm a reassuring squeeze before bustling off to handle the caffeine-deprived crowd, leaving me alone with my chaotic thoughts.

Taking the long way home, I absorb the peaceful serenity of Cedarwood. Trees line the streets, their leaves painting a portrait of autumn, a cascade of gold, amber, and fiery reds. The picturesque houses, most of them historic and charming, remind me of the home that has been in our family for generations.

Memories of childhood, playing in the yard, the sound of Mom's laughter, all pull at my heartstrings. The looming threat of losing it all is more than I can bear.

Max's proposition is absurd, tempting, terrifying, and alluring, all rolled into one giant mess. But it could also be the lifeline we so desperately need.

I pass the old bakery, the scent of freshly baked pastries wafting in the air, grounding me in the reality of my delightful hometown. What would a fake marriage with Max Decker do to this reality? And more importantly, what would it do to me?

As my house comes into view, with its slightly worn-out fence and the roses Mom loves so much, it's stately Victorian shape impressive as always, the question remains: am I ready to shake hands with a devil named Max to save it?

Sneaking through the front door, I'm immediately greeted by the thick, suffocating air of despair as Mom and Dad sit at the kitchen table, a cascade of bills, bank statements, and one very empty-looking checkbook spread before them.

They don't notice me right away, too consumed by the abysmal conversation they're submerged in. I linger for a moment, taking in the scene. Dad's rubbing the temples of his forehead, his usual robust complexion paler than the whitewash on the walls. Mom's eyes, always so lively and twinkling with mischief, are dimmed, holding back a reservoir of tears.

I inhale sharply, the sight stabbing through my heart like a frigid wind. They've always been the epitome of strength, the unwavering rocks of our family. Seeing them so fragile, so close to breaking... it's more than I can bear.

"I've got it all figured out here," Dad mumbles, his voice barely audible and coated with exhaustion. "If we can't conjure up some kind of miracle within the next two months, we..." He trails off, unable to put the inevitable into words.

Mom reaches across, placing a comforting hand on his. "We've been through worse, hon. We'll figure something out. We always do."

I take a step forward, my resolve hardening with each echo of their suffering. "That's not going to happen."

Three pairs of eyes meet—my parents' twinning in their surprise and a singular, fierce determination blazing in mine. I march to the table, hands planted firmly on the back of an empty chair, anchoring myself.

"We're not losing this house. I won't let that happen."

Mom blinks, a glimmer of hope flickering through her sadness. "Hailey, sweetheart, we can't expect you to—"

"Mom," I cut in, gently yet firmly, "you and Dad worked tirelessly to provide for Jake and me. You built a life, a home for us. Now it's my turn to help. I might have a solution."

The words hang in the air, a precarious offer laden with unseen consequences and a route fraught with unknowns. Yet, as I gaze into the weary eyes of the two most important people in my life, I realize that I'm willing to navigate through the stormiest of seas if it means preserving the sanctuary of our family.

Dad's eyes narrow slightly, a mix of curiosity and protective caution. "What are you talking about, kiddo?"

I inhale, a mix of dread and determination bubbling within me as the words tumble out, "I'm talking about getting us the money we need. I'm talking about a business deal."

"What kind of deal?" Mom asks.

"Just... just leave it to me."

I leave my parents sitting in bewildered silence, their faces a mosaic of shock, curiosity, and a sprinkle of fear. My heart is pounding a frenetic rhythm against my ribcage as I race up to my room, leaving the unfinished tale of my potential future swirling in the air behind me.

Once inside the familiar confines of my bedroom, I lean against the closed door, taking a shaky breath. My room has always been my sanctuary, a place where dreams took flight amidst posters of pop bands and shelves laden with well-loved books. But today, it feels different. The walls seem to echo with the ticking of an invisible clock, each second catapulting me toward a decision that could very well be my salvation—or my undoing.

I pivot on my heels and stride to the window, gazing out at the tapestry of Cedarwood spread below. It's peaceful, comforting... yet the glimmering lights from the Cedarwood Grand, the swanky hotel in the distance where Max is staying serve as a stark reminder of the reality awaiting me just a stone's throw away.

The room bathes in the waning sunlight, casting long shadows across the floor as I weigh the pros and cons of the ludicrous proposition lingering tantalizingly within reach.

Pro: Saving the house, the beautiful, memory-filled home that has been a steadfast constant throughout every chapter of my life.

Con: Binding myself, even momentarily, to Max Decker—the heartbreaker, the egotist, the man whose departure once left me nursing a wounded heart amidst shattered dreams.

Pro: Giving my parents the chance to breathe, to escape the crushing weight of impending financial ruin.

Con: Becoming tabloid fodder, the newest character in the never-ending drama that is Max Decker's love life.

The list goes on, each point a seesaw of practicality and emotion, tipping the scales in undetermined directions.

Glancing back toward the hotel, I see it not as a beacon of luxury, but as a symbol of solution—a way out of the mess that life has heaped at our doorstep. I think of my parents downstairs, poring over bills, their spirits breaking beneath the weight of insurmountable stress. The vision spurs something fierce and protective within me.

With a newfound resolve, I pull my hair back, tying it into a high ponytail, an armor of determination settling upon my shoulders. My reflection in the mirror stares back at me, eyes ablaze with a mix of defiance and challenge.

I'm Hailey Rogers, the girl who's spent her life shrouded in the comfort of predictability, always choosing the safest path.

But maybe, just maybe, it's time for me to be a little daring.

With one last steadying breath, I snatch my keys from the dresser and march determinedly toward the door, each step resounding with the echo of change.

The last thought that crosses my mind as I close the door behind me, embarking on a journey towards the unknown, is that I'm not doing this for Max, nor for the tantalizing web of faux romance that's about to unfurl. No, I'm doing this for them, for us—the family that's always been my anchor amidst life's tempests.

Max Decker, I'm coming for you, and I'm ready to play your game. But remember, I'm not the naive girl you once knew—I'm playing to win.

And with that thought, I step into the evening, ready to face whatever awaits.

12

Max

A RHYTHMIC TAPPING SLICES through my post-sauna serenity, drawing my eyes towards the door. I've wrapped a towel around my waist, and the last droplets of water are still sliding down my shoulders as I approach to answer it. This hotel is swanky enough not to bother guests without good cause, so whoever it is must have a damn good reason to interrupt my evening.

As I pull open the door, I'm greeted by a sight that's equally surprising and enticing: Hailey, standing in the hallway, her eyes wide and, dare I say, appreciative as they sweep over me.

"Oh... wow..." she mumbles, the color in her cheeks blossoming into a delightful shade of rose.

I lean against the doorframe, an eyebrow cocked and a sly grin curling on my lips. "As much as I enjoy being ogled, Rogers, I think it's customary to at least buy a guy dinner first."

Her eyes snap up to meet mine, the playful indignation in them sparking a warmth in my chest. Hailey folds her arms, unabashed.

"Believe me, Decker, if I wanted to ogle, I'd buy a ticket to one of your games."

I chuckle, stepping aside to allow her entrance. "Touché. Come on in."

While she steps into the lavish hotel room, I retreat to the bathroom, shedding my towel in favor of a pair of athletic shorts. I don't rush, taking a moment to appreciate the cool fabric against my skin and to fix my hair into a somewhat presentable state.

Emerging from the bathroom, I find Hailey perched on the edge of the plush bed, her fingers idly tracing the intricate patterns on the duvet. Her gaze lifts as I enter, flickering momentarily over my bare chest before she determinedly fixes her eyes on mine.

I can't resist a smirk, plopping down beside her, allowing our thighs to brush ever-so-slightly. "Alright, Rogers, I'm all ears. And eyes, apparently," I quip, nodding towards my torso.

She rolls her eyes but there's a playful lilt to her voice as she replies. "Keep dreaming, hotshot."

Despite the snark, I can see the seriousness pooling in her eyes, the way her fingers fidget nervously with the hem of her shirt. I tilt my head, letting the cocky exterior fade into genuine curiosity. "So, what brings you to my humble abode?"

Hailey takes a steadying breath, her fingers slightly trembling despite the boldness in her gaze. "Max," she begins, her voice a soft but sturdy whisper, "this is insane. You know it, I know it. There's about a million ways this could blow up in our faces... and yet, here I am."

She pauses, and I swear I can hear the quiet battle raging within her before she continues, "My parents... they're on the brink of losing everything. Our home, the place I grew up, it's teetering on the verge of becoming just another memory. And I can't—I won't—let that happen."

Hailey turns to me, her eyes reflecting a mixture of vulnerability and iron-willed resolve. "So, yeah, your crazy plan? Your ticket out of the doghouse with the media, your sponsors, and whoever else? It just might be my ticket to saving my family's home."

A bitter laugh escapes her, punctuating the silence that hangs heavily between us. "A fake engagement to Max Decker, the heartthrob hockey player of Cedarwood High, the man who sauntered back into town with the chaos of a love triangle tailing him... Who would've thought?"

She leans in slightly, her voice dropping to an earnest, almost pleading whisper. "But if we do this, Max, if I agree to be your... whatever... you need to promise me something."

Her eyes pierce into mine, unwavering, as she utters her non-negotiable terms. "Promise me that no matter what happens, my parents will never find out about this deal. Promise me that the story we sell to the world won't tarnish them or our town. And promise me that when it all falls apart—and it will, Max, because fake things always do—the backlash won't drag them down with us."

"And," Hailey puffs out, with a half-exasperated, half-amused roll of her eyes, "will you please put on a damn shirt?"

I let a slow, mischievous grin crawl across my face. "Why, Hailey Rogers, is my semi-nude physique proving to be too much of a distraction for you?"

Despite the quip, her cheeks don't flare with the anticipated blush. Instead, she sends a playful but pointed look my way, one eyebrow quirked upwards. Point for Rogers.

I yield, snatching a shirt off a nearby chair and pulling it over my head, not without giving her a wink that just slightly tugs at the corner of her mouth. My eyes linger a moment too long on her—those snug jeans, a blouse that's casual yet somehow alluring as it drapes over her, and damn, if she doesn't wear autumn like a second skin. Effortlessly, unassumingly hot.

I clear my throat and pull myself back into the conversation, locking eyes with her. "Alright, Hailey, you have my word. Your parents, they won't know a thing about our deal. I'll protect them—and you—from any fallout."

Nodding, more to myself than her, I continue, "And I'll do one better. After the sponsors are back and I'm the prodigal son returned in the media's eyes, I'll do a whole 'Max Decker gives back to his hometown' circus. We'll lump in a hefty amount for your parents as part of a donation drive or something. No one will be the wiser."

The compliment must have landed, as she surveys me, seemingly peeling back the layers of the notorious playboy to see if, beneath all the façade and show, there's a sliver of sincerity. "Max, you've got shrewd down to an art form."

I spread my arms wide, bowing theatrically in my hotel room. "What can I say? It's a gift."

Her arms cross, but the atmosphere between us lightens, just a fraction. "You've done this before, haven't you? Bent the narrative to save your skin?"

Now it's my turn to be scrutinized, and I sustain her gaze, my response a shrug laced with candor. "Not quite like this. Hailey, I've twisted truths, played the media, sure. But this—" I gesture between us, encompassing the charged air, the impending chaos we're stepping into "—this is uncharted territory."

We sit in that confessional silence, the acknowledgment of our impending storm hanging heavily between us. Then, with a quiet strength, she utters, "We're doing this, aren't we?"

And there's nothing left to say, because yes, we're plummeting headfirst into this wild, reckless plot, together. And in that agreement, amidst the looming chaos, there's a bizarre unity, an alliance forged in desperation, in audacity, and hell, maybe a dash of insane courage.

With that, we dive into it, ordering some takeout and starting our brainstorming session for just how this plan's going to look.

The smell of Chinese takeout soon fills the room, a mix of sweet, spicy, and savory wafting between us as we hash out the absurd details of our soon-to-be mock engagement. Our plan scribbles sprawl across the hotel notepad, a roadmap to the most ludicrous journey either of us have embarked on.

We cover the basics, all right. The "how-we-fell-back-in-love" story for the press, a timeline of our romance rekindling, the proposal—appropriately public and heart-meltingly sweet, of course—, and all those tiny, authentic details that'll make even the most skeptical hearts swoon.

Hours blur into one another, and our scheming is punctuated by bites of Kung Pao chicken and vegetable fried rice. Eventually, our plan takes enough shape that I can see this crazy scheme just might work. It's in the sassy tilt of Hailey's eyebrows and the amused curve of her lips that I recognize a mirrored thrill at our daring.

Eventually, I order some wine, a fancy red blend, delivered by room service with two gleaming glasses.

"To..." I start, swirling the ruby liquid in my glass, "to the craziest damn thing we've ever done?"

Hailey chuckles, a rich, warm sound that buzzes pleasantly in the space between us. Her glass chinks gently against mine. "To jumping off cliffs and building our wings on the way down."

A thoughtful silence pools between us as we sip, and I'm caught in a maelstrom of contemplation, observing how the soft glow of the room lights casts a gentle sheen on her dark hair.

She breaks the quiet, her voice a bemused whisper, "Can you believe this, Max? I mean, really believe it?"

"Not in a million years."

She shifts, folding one leg beneath her, her demeanor flitting between playful and soberingly serious. Her eyes flicker, pausing on my lips for the briefest of moments before dancing back to meet my gaze.

"And... the PDA?" Her voice quivers just slightly, betraying the nonchalant mask. "How do we... navigate that?"

"The what?" I ask.

"You know, PDA—public displays of affection."

I lean back, the leather of the sofa creaking beneath me, and scrutinize her. "We wing it. Keep it light, natural. No need to put on a Broadway show, we just need to be convincing enough."

I lean forward, elbows on knees, and clear my throat awkwardly, which is kind of a novel experience because 'awkward' is not typically in my vocabulary.

"Hailey, we should, uh, practice. The PDA thing, I mean."

She tilts her head, one perfect brow arching upward. "Practice?"

"Yes, practice," I affirm, locking my jaw in a mock-serious pose. "You know, so it doesn't look like we're two actors poorly cast in some cringy romantic comedy."

She mulls this over, then shakes her head with a light, unbelieving laugh. "This is insane, Decker."

"Ah, but it's our insanity," I reply, stretching my arm across the back of the sofa, an invitation hanging silently in the air.

She accepts, sliding closer, tucking neatly under my arm, her head finding a place to rest on my shoulder. Her hair brushes against my skin, soft and fragrant, throwing my senses into a quiet kind of chaos.

This was a bad idea. A horrifically, astonishingly bad idea.

Her warmth seeps through the fabric of my shirt, a slow burn, as I'm consumed by a fire of memories and 'what-ifs.' My hand absentmindedly settles on her waist, tracing the curve of her hip through the fabric of her blouse.

"Comfortable?" My voice is a whisper, barely daring to ripple through the atmosphere we've cocooned ourselves in.

She hums affirmatively, fingers playing with the hem of my shirt. A soft, contemplative silence veils us, and I wonder if she's as trapped by memories of us as I am.

Then, she says it.

"We should probably practice kissing, too."

My heart stutters, lurches, races. But I keep my voice even. "Smart. Can't have people thinking it's our first rodeo."

We pivot toward each other, the air thickening, and my breath hitches as her hand gently cradles my jaw. Her eyes are oceans, and I'm drowning, willingly sinking into their depths.

Our lips meet, a whisper of a touch, and every resolve, every erected wall crumbles beneath the softness of her kiss.

We said practice, but this isn't practice. It's a remembrance, a revival of every unsaid word, every suppressed feeling, every moment where our paths diverged and converged in the chaotic dance that's been our history.

My hand weaves into her hair, her body presses closer, and the practice fades into genuineness. It's gentle yet ravenous, sweet yet scalding, a complex contradiction that has always defined 'us.'

As we break apart, our foreheads rest against each other, breath mingling, reality tugging us back from the precipice we dared to dance upon.

My voice is ragged, almost lost amidst the thundering of my heart. "That was..."

"Yeah," she agrees, not moving, her breath a warm caress against my lips.

A calamity of emotions storms through me, and I know, without a shred of doubt, that this sham of an engagement is going to be anything but simple.

Shit.

13

Hailey

Goddamnit.

The world around me seems to blur, the periphery fading into nothingness as those stormy blue eyes of Max's anchor me to the here and now. Holy crap. Kissing Max? Again? Didn't see that one coming.

"Wow, Decker," I manage to get out, taking a shaky breath, "I didn't expect the practice run to be this... intense."

His smirk is as intoxicating as the kiss we just shared. "You think I've lost my touch?"

I laugh, but it's a breathless sound. A mere pretense covering the electricity that's crackling between us. "That was... nostalgic."

He raises an eyebrow, challenging. "Only nostalgic?"

Damn him and his knowing smirks. But two can play this game. "Perhaps a tad familiar," I admit, biting my lower lip, eyes dancing with mischief.

In a heartbeat, we're at it again, lips locked, hands wandering, pulling each other closer as if magnetically drawn. With every inch of closing space, with every stolen breath, the outside world continues to fade away.

"Bad idea," I gasp between kisses, feeling his hands slide down my back, pulling me even closer.

"Terrible," he agrees, his voice husky, but there's a glint of mischief in his eyes that matches my own.

In a whirlwind of motion and sensation, my hands are on his chest, fingertips grazing his skin as I pull off his shirt. Why did I do that? Well, let's not question impulsiveness. The warmth of his skin under my hands is distracting, and the way his muscles ripple... I'm not sure if I want to slap him or keep touching.

"You've been working out," I remark, eyebrows raised in feigned surprise, even as my fingers trace the lines of his abs.

He chuckles, the sound low and teasing. "Perks of the job. You noticed?"

"Oh, believe me, it's hard not to." I reply, trying to keep my voice even, though my heart is racing.

There's a pause, our eyes locked, the playful banter a mere cover for the unspoken tension that stretches taut between us. I want to pull back, to draw a line, to create boundaries. But in that moment, there's no room for rational thought. The only thing that matters is this magnetic pull between us.

"I should stop," I whisper, even as I lean in, drawn to him like a moth to a flame.

"Me too," he murmurs, but his lips find mine once more, erasing any semblance of restraint.

Deep down, we both know this is a dangerous game, blurring the lines of our agreement. But in this heated moment, none of that matters. All that exists is us and the undeniable connection we share.

The rhythmic thumping of my heart feels almost deafening in the silence of the room. With every press of his lips, every stolen breath, the world shrinks until it's just me and Max, our past and present colliding in a whirlwind of sensation.

Every touch, every brush of skin on skin, feels electrifying, magnified a thousand times over. It's been years since high school. But right now, it's like I'm seventeen all over again, feeling that giddy excitement of a first crush—only more potent, more intense.

Max's fingers deftly work the buttons on my shirt, revealing the skin underneath. He tugs it off, along with my bra, leaving me exposed. And for a moment, I feel a pang of vulnerability, but then his eyes meet mine, and it's not just lust I see, it's admiration, wonder, and a hint of that familiar mischief.

I can't help but grin, that schoolgirl-ish, cheeky smile that always got me into trouble. "You sure you can handle this, Decker?" I tease.

His response is a confident smirk, his thumb tracing the curve of my collarbone. "Always could, always will."

The air between us is thick with memories, with the weight of all the things left unsaid over the years. But none of that matters now. We're here, drawn together once again by that undeniable pull.

His mouth is on mine, and I can't help but get lost in the rhythm of our lips moving together. My fingers find their way to his hair, tangling in those dark strands, pulling him even closer. The feeling of his skin, warm and tight against mine, is nothing short of addictive.

It's surreal, this mix of familiarity and discovery. The Max I remember was a boy full of swagger and charm, always ready with a quick comeback or a cheeky grin. But the man before me now? He's more, so much more. He's the sum of all his experiences, all the heartbreaks, and triumphs, and it only makes him all the more irresistible.

Lying there, bare and vulnerable, everything becomes a tantalizing game of sensations. The room, filled with the steady thrum of anticipation, seems to shimmer with an unspoken electricity. Each touch, each brush of skin against skin, sends ripples of pleasure coursing through me. It's as if we're dancing on the edge of a precipice, the thrill of the unknown beckoning us forward.

Max's movements are deliberate, confident. And with one swift motion, I find myself looking up at the ceiling, lying on my back with the edge of the bed beneath me. Those stormy blue eyes of his bore into mine, teasing and testing.

He grins, that mischievous, devil-may-care grin that always promised trouble back in high school. And as he maneuvers between my legs, easing them onto his broad shoulders, I'm reminded of why I always found that grin so irresistible.

"You know," he starts, voice dripping with playful confidence, "our little rendezvous all those years ago? There was something I always wished I'd done."

I raise an eyebrow, challenging him. "Oh? And what's that?"

He leans in, his lips brushing against my ear, sending shivers down my spine. "I always wondered what you tasted like."

His boldness takes me off guard, the audacity of his words making my heart race. It's that same Max—always pushing the boundaries, always making me question my own limits. Yet, as audacious as his words are, they're also... inviting.

He doesn't wait for a response, his mouth soon exploring, leaving a trail of heat wherever it lands. The sensation is electrifying. Each touch, each kiss pulls me deeper, blurring the lines between past and present. It feels like a trip down memory lane and a venture into new territory all at once.

His fingers trace the contour of my cheek, his touch setting my skin aflame. "Hailey," he says, voice dripping with passion "how is it possible for a woman to be this captivating?"

I raise an eyebrow, trying to keep my composure, "Going for the full Casanova today, are we?"

He smirks, a playful glint in his eyes. "When in Rome—or in this case, when with the most enchanting woman I've ever laid eyes on."

Max's gaze travels over me, every look laden with admiration. "Every detail of you, from these tantalizing lips," he leans in, grazing his own against them, "to the allure of your curves," his hands daring to venture further.

Flattery warms my cheeks. "Max, any more of this talk and you'll have me believing I'm some sort of goddess."

His grin is devilish, but his eyes are sincere. "Isn't that the truth? Every time I see you, it's like witnessing a stunning sunset—breathtaking, unique, and impossible to resist."

It's my turn to smirk. "Been reading those old romance novels again?"

He chuckles, a throaty sound that makes my pulse quicken. "Maybe, but only because they seem to be the only thing that comes close to capturing your essence."

I pretend to ponder, tapping my chin. "Hmm, always the charmer, aren't you?"

His wink is pure mischief. "Only for you, gorgeous."

The reality is, his gaze, his words, have always had this power over me. It's not just the lust in his eyes—it's the reverence. The way he admires every inch of me, as though my body is an artwork, one he's privileged to behold. His focus particularly lingers on my breasts, each glance filled with animal lust.

I can't help but be acutely aware of my imperfections—the little stretch marks, the way I've changed over the years—but instead of making me feel self-conscious, it's as if he's cherishing each unique mark, each story my skin tells.

The world outside blurs as the intimacy between us intensifies. Every touch, every whispered compliment deepens the bond, making our past and the present moment seem intertwined.

With him, I feel celebrated, accepted—loved, even. It's a sensation that feels both new and familiar, and it overwhelms me.

Then, Max's body aligns with mine, his warm weight pressing down, filling the space around me, as he finally moves closer, forging our connection even more deeply. He pushes inside, my pussy so wet by this point that he easily enters me.

"Oh... Oh God."

He grins, clearly taking pleasure in the effect he has on me. I squirm underneath him as he pushes inside, his thickness stretching me out. My nails dig into the thick, powerful muscles of his upper back as he bottoms me out all of the way. When he's filled me full, I feel as if I might melt.

"That feel good?" he asks.

"You've got no freaking idea."

He laughs, then his expression turns serious as he pulls back and drives into me again, over and over. Each penetration is easier than the last, my walls stretching to accommodate his size. We move together, Max leaning down and kissing me hard, his tongue dancing with mine as the steady pace of his hips guides me to orgasm.

A heady rush of warmth radiates from my core, spreading outwards like ripples in water. Every inch of me tightens, then shudders with release. An intense wave of pleasure sweeps over me, consuming every thought, every breath, as I succumb to the exquisite sensation.

He groans as I come, his cock throbbing inside as he releases, his hot seed shooting deeply inside. We freeze together in climax, my scream cut short as he grunts hard, pumping into me hard a few more times before relenting and falling to my side.

Lying there, the cool sheets tangled around our bodies, the afterglow feels like a soft hum in the air, echoing the remnants of our escapade. My heartbeat hasn't yet caught up with reality, thumping loudly in my chest, making me acutely aware of the warm body next to mine. The ceiling seems to pulsate slightly, or perhaps it's just my head, spinning from the rush of emotions.

A tidal wave of thoughts crashes against my consciousness. Was this what I signed up for? The room's dim lighting doesn't hide the reality of the situation, and I can still feel the heat of Max's gaze on my skin. Out of the corner of my eye, I can see his signature smirk, that look of smug satisfaction plastered across his face. Damn him.

"It's funny," I muse aloud, but mostly to myself, "how a simple arrangement can quickly spiral into..." I wave my hand around vaguely, trying to capture the whirlwind essence of what just unfolded.

Max chuckles, his deep laugh sending a tingle down my spine. "Into this?"

I shoot him a glance. "Yes, this," I stress, as if he's been entirely clueless about the proceedings.

He props himself up on one elbow, turning to face me, his grin now wider than ever. "Can't say I saw it coming, but I'm not complaining."

The reality of it all sinks in, and the weight of what's transpired becomes too much to bear silently.

Turning to him, I blurt out, "Seriously, what the HELL just happened?"

Max's eyebrows shoot up in mock surprise. "I thought that was pretty self-explanatory."

I narrow my eyes, not in the mood for his cheekiness. "I meant... us. This isn't part of the deal, Max."

He chuckles, but there's a softness in his voice, a hint of uncertainty. "Look, Hailey," he begins, tracing circles on my arm. "I won't pretend to know what just happened either, but I do know it felt... right. Like everything just clicked into place."

I turn to face him, our gazes locking, searching for answers. Was this just a fluke, a mistake? Or had we been ignoring something real between us all these years? But the real question is, what now?

A million questions whirl around in my head, and while I wish for answers, I know we have a bigger game at play. With the stakes so high, can we afford to get lost in whatever this is?

Sighing, I pull the sheets tighter around me. "We need to set some boundaries, Max. We can't afford distractions."

Max chuckles again. "Oh, sorry. Was I a distraction?"

"Oh, shut up."

14

Max

There's a newfound stillness between us. It's like the world's taken a deep breath, just waiting for Hailey to let it out. She pushes herself upright, the sheets pooling around her waist, and I take a sneaky moment to appreciate the view. Determination sets her features, eyes blazing like she's prepped for battle. I find it kinda hot. And kinda terrifying.

"Max," she starts, pointing an accusing finger in my direction. "What just happened... it was a mistake. A slip-up. We're in this for one reason and one reason only, remember?"

I nod, letting her words settle, but I can't resist the urge to tease. My eyes dart down to her chest, and then I glance back up, a smirk playing on my lips. "Sorry, was distracted for a sec. Could you repeat that last bit?"

The sound she makes is half growl, half exasperated sigh. A pillow flies at my head, and I just manage to duck out of the way. Laughing, I watch as she gets to her feet, gathering her clothes with that same determined focus.

"Real mature, Max," she mutters, snatching her panties off the ground and angrily stepping into them.

"I mean, c'mon, Hales," I counter, sitting up and letting the sheets fall away. "I was just having a bit of fun. I was listening. Mostly."

She eyes me warily, as she buttons up her blouse. "You promise?"

Running a hand through my hair, I give her my most sincere look. "Yeah, yeah, I promise. I got the message loud and clear. We keep it professional. No more... distractions."

She narrows her eyes, clearly debating if she can trust me. "Good," she finally says. "Because this is too important to screw up."

I nod, swinging my legs over the edge of the bed. "I get it, Hailey. I'm on board."

We share a moment of understanding, two comrades ready to face whatever comes next. But beneath it all, I can't help but wonder if we can really put this genie back in its bottle. Whatever happened between us felt electric, and I have a sneaking suspicion that it's not going to be easy to forget.

Hailey's still in full lecture mode, hands flitting as she talks. "Seriously. We have to remain professional, Max. We cannot let these... indiscretions happen."

I raise an eyebrow at the word 'indiscretions.' But who am I to argue semantics? Instead, I'm having a tough time keeping my gaze from wandering, watching the smooth movement of her arms and the sway of her hips as she talks. The way she shimmies into her jeans is positively hypnotic—just effortlessly hot.

"Max!" she snaps, catching me in the act.

"Sorry, Hales," I say with a grin, holding my hands up in surrender. "But you really do look as good putting clothes on as you do taking them off."

She shoots me a look, a mix of exasperation and amusement. "God, you're impossible. Do you even understand what I'm saying? This was a huge slip-up!"

I stretch my arms out, leaning back against the headboard. "Oh, I get it. But, honestly? I think it's no biggie."

Her face scrunches in confusion. "No biggie? Max, we—"

"Hooked up. Yeah, I was there," I cut her off, winking. "And it was fantastic, by the way."

"That's not the point," she huffs. "We can't afford distractions, especially not... this kind of distraction."

Laughing, I run a hand through my hair. "Look, we've got history. That's just a fact. It's part of what makes this whole charade believable, right? And with history like ours, there's gonna be some... residual tension."

She crosses her arms, skepticism etched on her face. "Residual tension?"

"Oh, come on," I counter with a chuckle. "You can't tell me you didn't feel it, too. The spark. The... magnetism. It was bound to get in the way eventually."

She tilts her head, mulling over my words. "So, you're saying...?"

"That we got it out of our system," I finish for her, smirking. "We broke the tension. Now, we can move on and focus on the task at hand. No more wondering 'what if.' We know. It was hot. End of story."

She blinks, processing. After a moment, she lets out a shaky laugh, rubbing her forehead. "Max, only you could spin this situation into something positive."

I shrug, grinning. "What can I say? It's a talent."

She shakes her head, smiling despite herself. "You're ridiculous."

"And you love it," I retort, wiggling my eyebrows.

She laughs again, the tension between us finally dissipating. "Yeah, yeah. Just... let's keep it in our pants from now on, okay?"

"No promises," I tease, winking. "But I'll try my best."

Hailey rolls her eyes, but I catch the hint of a smile playing at the corners of her mouth. For now, at least, crisis averted.

Hailey shifts her weight, casting a pointed glance at my still very undressed form. "There's a lot we need to discuss, you know."

I cock an eyebrow at her, my grin shamelessly wide. "Like what?"

She stifles a chuckle, indicating the very evident fact of my lack of attire. "Well, for starters, maybe you could put some clothes on?"

"Fine," I feign disappointment, my grin unrelenting, "but no peeking, alright?"

She rolls her eyes, the playful exasperation evident. "Trust me, I've seen enough."

"Hardly," I laugh, winking at her.

But as I start to dress, pulling on my shorts, I can't help but feel the weight of her gaze. I can practically hear the gears in her head turning, planning the next step in our little arrangement. She begins to speak, and I glance over my shoulder, catching her eyes darting away from my torso.

"I thought we said 'no peeking'," I remark, the playful tone dripping in my voice.

"Whatever," she huffs, her cheeks betraying her with a hint of blush.

She clears her throat, finding her composure again. "Alright, so about sharing the news with the world. Look, I might not be an influencer or whatever they call it, but I've learned a thing or two from the zoomer interns at work."

I tug a shirt over my head, suddenly grateful she isn't suggesting I become a TikTok sensation. "Zoomers, huh? Well, enlighten me."

She leans back, hands on hips, thinking for a moment. "Well, for starters, subtlety is key. It's not about making a huge announcement or putting out some overly-posed photos. The trick is to get people talking, speculating."

I nod in agreement. "So, a gradual reveal?"

"Exactly!" She enthuses, animatedly. "We can start by appearing in each other's stories—nothing direct, just glimpses. And maybe a photo or two where we're in the background together, but not the main focus. Let the eagle-eyed fans connect the dots."

I laugh at the idea of 'eagle-eyed fans' dissecting our every move, but I can't deny she has a point. "Sounds sneaky. I like it."

Her lips twitch upwards. "And then there's the issue of comments. We'll have to play along with the speculations, maybe leave some flirty comments on each other's posts. But nothing too blatant. The interns call this a soft launch."

"Flirty comments?" I smirk. "I think I can handle that."

Hailey quirks an eyebrow, her lips curving into a teasing smile. "Oh, I'm sure you can. Just try not to overdo it, Casanova."

"I'll have you know, I am the perfect amount of flirt," I boast, puffing out my chest.

She lets out a genuine laugh, pointing a finger at me. "That's the spirit. Just remember, it's all a game. And the aim is to keep them guessing, keep them talking."

I flex dramatically, posing. "Baby, with us? They'll never stop talking."

Hailey chuckles, shaking her head at my antics. "Alright, show-off. Just remember our plan, and no going rogue on me."

I salute her mockingly. "Aye aye, Captain."

As she chuckles, I can't help but feel a strange mix of excitement and trepidation. This whole thing might be crazier than I'd ever imagined, but with Hailey by my side, I can't deny the thrill of the chase. Let the games begin.

15

Hailey

THE CITY IS JUST waking up when I head over to Max's place. Morning light filters softly through the trees, casting a warm golden hue on the pavements. It's that in-between time when the city's usual bustling noises are on pause, and for a moment, everything feels serene. Perfect for planning a relationship launch—well, at least the fake kind.

I knock on Max's door, balancing a tray of coffee in one hand and a thick binder stuffed with notes and ideas in the other. After a minute, the door creaks open to reveal a very disheveled Max, hair sticking up in every direction and sleep still evident in his eyes.

"Morning, sunshine!" I chirp, offering him one of the coffees.

He squints against the morning light. "It's criminal to be up this early," he mumbles, accepting the coffee with a grunt. "What's got you so wired?"

"I've been up since five," I confess. "Did you know there's this whole science to social media relationship reveals? Timing, content type, frequency—it's like a whole other world!"

He raises an eyebrow, sipping his coffee. "Should've known you'd go full Hermione Granger on this. Some things never change."

"And some people never learn to become morning people." I wink, stepping past him into his living room. I'm met with the delightful mess of his life—clothes strewn about, random protein shake containers, and, for some reason, a lone dumbbell next to his couch. "Still the neat freak I see."

He chuckles, following me inside. "Well, not all of us have color-coded planners and alarms set for ungodly hours."

I set my binder on his coffee table, flinging it open to a page marked "Step One." The table quickly becomes a maze of color-coded tabs, Post-its, and highlighters.

Max, now more awake, whistles lowly. "Is this the plan for our relationship or a plan to invade a small country?"

"Funny," I shoot back with a smirk, "But seriously, I think I've cracked the code. We need teaser posts, candid shots, strategically timed stories. Oh, and definitely a weekend trip photo series. People eat that stuff up."

He lounges on his sofa, still nursing his coffee, clearly entertained by my enthusiasm. "You've really outdone yourself, Granger. Ready to teach this old dog some new tricks?"

I give him a playful shove. "Only if this 'old dog' is ready to cooperate. We've got a busy few weeks ahead."

His smile is genuine, appreciative. "Alright, lay it on me. Let's make the world believe in 'us'."

The living room is awash with colors from my plethora of sticky notes, tabs, and highlighters. I take a deep breath, gathering my thoughts. Max lounges on his couch, watching me with a mix of amusement and intrigue. This feels like one of our college cram sessions, and the nostalgia isn't lost on either of us.

"Alright," I begin, leaning over the coffee table and tapping on a sheet labeled 'Objective.' "The goal of our soft launch is to subtly introduce our relationship to the public in a way that feels authentic. Think of it as a sneak peek, like dropping breadcrumbs for our audience to follow. We're creating a narrative."

Max tilts his head, taking a sip of his now lukewarm coffee. "Narrative? So we're storytellers now?"

"In a way, yes. The story needs to be convincing for the public to buy our engagement." I flip to a pie chart filled with different colors, each representing a social media platform. "Each platform serves a purpose. Instagram for visuals, Twitter for conversations and, of course, Facebook for those older family members and friends."

He chuckles. "I didn't realize fake dating would be so complicated."

I shoot him a smirk. "That's because you've got me at the helm, steering this ship. And it's crucial we get this right because the soft launch sets the tone for everything that follows. If we make it believable now, the actual engagement announcement will be easier to swallow. People love a good love story, and we're giving it to them piece by piece."

Max nods, beginning to grasp the importance. "So, what's the game plan?"

I show him a timeline filled with different posts, dates, and captions. "We start with a few vague posts—maybe a shared sunset with a cryptic caption, progress to posting photos together at events, but not too posed. We want it to seem candid and natural. And we'll occasionally share glimpses of our dates."

He raises an eyebrow. "Dates?"

I nod. "Fake ones. Like, dinner at home or a movie night. We want to look smitten but not overly showy."

Max chuckles, "Alright, sounds doable. Anything else?"

"Yes." I look him straight in the eyes, "You need to be a good boy."

His eyes sparkle with mischief. "Oh, I'm always good. In fact, some might say I'm exceptionally good."

I'm not falling for his playful tone. "I mean it, Max. No flirting with random women, no mysterious late-night outings. If there's even a hint that you're not 100% devoted to me, it'll be a PR disaster. Our story has to be airtight."

He holds his hands up in surrender. "Got it, boss. Only have eyes for you." He mock salutes, making me chuckle.

But I want to make sure he gets the gravity of it. "Seriously, Max. No slip-ups. We're in this together, and if one of us falters, it affects both of us."

He nods, the smirk fading, replaced by a genuine look of understanding. "I got it, Hailey. You have my word."

I sigh in relief. "Good. Now, let's dive into the details and make everyone believe in our epic love story."

The room is thick with the whirring of my thoughts, and I can practically see the wheels turning in Max's head. He's always been quick on the uptake, which is both endearing and infuriating.

"Alright, the first thing we're going to tackle is the mystery of our 'dates'," I start, fingers making quotation marks in the air.

Max tilts his head, confusion evident. "Mystery dates? Why can't we just, you know, post a picture of us together?"

I chuckle, shaking my head. "Too obvious. Remember, we're dropping breadcrumbs. The audience should feel like they're cleverly piecing things together."

He narrows his eyes, leaning back into the couch with a smirk. "So, cryptic but not too cryptic?"

"Exactly," I nod, impressed. "Like maybe a shot of a beautiful beach picnic setting with just a hint of a woman's hand, complete with polished nails, in the frame. Makes them wonder, 'Who's that with Max?'"

His grin widens. "I've always been a huge fan of mysterious lunches, especially when they come with pretty hands."

I raise an eyebrow, feigning disapproval. "Focus, Max. This isn't a joke."

He chuckles, holding his hands up in mock surrender. "Alright, alright, I'm all ears. Tell me more about this mysterious date."

I think for a moment, scanning my mental map of Cedarwood. "How about Crystal Cove? It's a charming beachside location and pretty secluded. Plus, the name sounds magical, doesn't it?"

He nods, looking genuinely excited. "I love it. A picnic on Crystal Cove it is. What's on the menu?"

"I'm thinking of getting something from Lucy's coffee shop. She makes the best charcuterie plates in town. Plus, it's bound to look as delicious in photos as it tastes."

Max's eyes practically light up at the mention of charcuterie. "Count me in. I remember stealing bits from your plate back in the day."

"Hey, those were my olives!" I tease, wagging a finger at him.

He laughs, and for a second, the world feels like a simpler place. "So, when is our date?"

"Be ready at 5 PM sharp—we need to be there in time for the setting sun. No excuses. I'll handle the rest," I command, with a little playful authority.

He mock salutes. "Aye aye, captain!"

"Just one more thing," I add with a sly grin.

His eyebrow arches in response, waiting.

"Dress to get wet," I quip, my smile mysterious.

He blinks, then chuckles, the rich sound filling the room. "Wet? Well, that's intriguing. I'm game, but I expect a proper explanation when the time comes."

I wink, gathering my things. "Just making sure our 'soft launch' is splashy enough. See you in a bit, Max."

16

Max

THE DIMMED LIGHTS OF a rooftop bar cast sultry shadows everywhere. Hailey, in a daring crimson number that hugs her silhouette perfectly, slowly walks over. Her heels click in a hypnotic rhythm against the marble floor, turning every head in the room, but her eyes are locked onto mine. As she draws closer, the noise around us fades, leaving just the two of us in a world of our own.

My hand instinctively reaches for her waist, pulling her close. There's a tease of a smile playing on her lips as she tilts her face upwards, eyes half-lidded, mouth slightly parted. Anticipation thickens the air—

The reality that I'm still in my hotel room crashes back with the insistence of my phone's shrill ringtone. Annoyance flares within me as I wrestle with the device. The caller ID flashes "Larry."

Rubbing the bridge of my nose, I take a breath and answer. "Lawrence, impeccable timing as always."

"That's what I'm here for," he responds drily. "You missed our catch-up, Max. Spill."

Rolling my eyes, I say, "Had a change in plans. We're about to announce a fake engagement with Hailey Rogers, starting with a 'soft launch' on social media."

Lawrence huffs, audibly irritated. "A 'soft what' now? Social media? Why complicate things? In my day, a press release did the job just fine."

Chuckling, I quip, "Well, Lawrence, times have changed. In a few hours, we'll have a beachside picnic pic floating around. You can even check out our Instagram story if you're feeling adventurous."

There's an exasperated sigh from the other end. "I swear, social media is the end of true PR. But fine, I'll bite. Why Hailey Rogers?"

"I have my reasons," I reply vaguely. "Let's just say it benefits both of us."

Lawrence's skepticism is clear. "You're playing a high-stakes game here. I hope you know what you're doing. And for heaven's sake, Max, try to keep this 'engagement' out of the tabloids until you're ready to officially announce it."

I laugh, "Worried about your reputation, are we?"

"Always," he retorts. "You might play fast and loose with yours, but I've worked hard to maintain mine. Don't make me regret taking you on as a client."

The threat behind his words is clear, but I'm undeterred. "Trust me, Lawrence. I've got this under control."

"We'll see," he grumbles. "Just remember: I'll be keeping an eye out for that Instagram story of yours."

"You do that," I say, chuckling. "Until then."

We hang up, and I flop back onto my bed. From a heated rendezvous with Hailey to a lecture from Lawrence in the span of minutes. What a rollercoaster.

But as I contemplate the adventure that lies ahead, excitement bubbles up again. The game is on, and I'm all in.

The thought of Hailey's words, "dress to get wet," plays in my mind like a catchy tune that refuses to go away. If I'm dressing for the potential of water, surely she is too, right? The image of Hailey in a form-fitting swimsuit, sun glinting off her damp skin, sauntering out of the waves like some modern-day Venus, invades my thoughts.

I can picture the droplets of seawater making rivulets down her shapley arms and legs, her laughter light and infectious as she challenges me to another impromptu dip in the ocean. I feel the tension rise—honestly, how does she manage to be so damn distracting?

Buzz! My phone vibrates, ending the tantalizing daydream. A text from Hailey lights up the screen. Don't be late for our 'date,' playboy.

I smirk, quickly typing a response. Not to worry, darling. I wouldn't dream of keeping you waiting. After all, the thought of what awaits at our seaside rendezvous has me more than a little eager.

Scanning my closet, I look for something effortlessly casual yet suitable for the occasion. My fingers brush a light, short-sleeved shirt, perfect for the beach. Pairing it with some comfortable shorts, I remember to grab a towel—just in case the "getting wet" wasn't metaphorical. Slipping on my well-worn boat shoes and grabbing a pair of shades, I give myself a once-over in the mirror. Easy, breezy beach day Max. Perfect.

Cedarwood in fall is nothing short of picturesque—the trees adorned in hues of gold, amber, and rust, their leaves dancing to the song of the gentle wind. But today, it's the beach that calls. As I walk out, the slightly warm sun graces my skin. The kind of warmth that reminds you of a perfect summer's day, even when the calendar tells you it's fall.

Starting my Ferrari, I relish the rumble of the engine. The drive to our chosen beach spot isn't long, but the anticipation makes it feel like an eternity. Cedarwood's coastline comes into view, the waves frothy and inviting, crashing against the sand, which sparkles under the day's light. Beachgoers, a mix of locals and tourists, dot the landscape, but I can spot Hailey from a mile away. She's busy setting up the perfect picnic spot. Her determination is honestly adorable.

As I park, the tantalizing aroma of the nearby food stalls fills the air—grilled seafood, freshly baked pastries, the kind of smells that make you forget about beach bodies and diets. But even those mouthwatering scents don't distract me from the sight of Hailey.

Pulling the car keys from the ignition, I take a deep breath. Here's to the start of our "soft launch."

As I approach the beach, the scene before me is straight out of a romance novel. A delicate breeze carries the tang of the ocean, ruffling Hailey's hair as she sits poised like a siren amidst a Pinterest-perfect setting. An intricately patterned beach blanket is spread on the sand, and in the center, a charcuterie board worthy of a gourmet magazine cover. There's everything from cheeses and fruits to crackers and some kind of jam I can't quite identify but looks mouthwateringly good.

She looks up, a hint of annoyance flashing in her eyes, and I instantly know I'm in trouble. "You're late," she points out, one brow raised in playful reproach.

Glancing at my Patek Philippe, the minute hand just past its mark, I counter, "Two minutes. You're counting two minutes? Come on, Hailey, even my coaches don't get on my case for a mere 120 seconds."

She stands up, dusting sand off her sundress, and shoots me a look. "This isn't hockey practice, Max. When I say eleven on the dot, I mean eleven on the dot. Your superstar charms may work with your coaches, but they don't fly here."

I can't help but chuckle, thoroughly enjoying her feisty energy. "You know, most would consider two minutes fashionably late."

Rolling her eyes with a sigh, she replies, "Fashionably late doesn't apply to dates, even fake ones. Especially when we're trying to convince the world of our budding 'romance.' You respect me too much to pull these kinds of shenanigans. After all, I'm supposed to be the girl whose love puts you on the straight and narrow, right?"

I smirk, holding my hands up in surrender. "Okay, okay, point taken. I'll set three alarms next time, just for you."

We both share a brief laugh, the tension easing. The waves roll in, playing their soothing symphony in the background, as gulls cry overhead, dancing in the warm fall breeze.

With a graceful gesture towards our beautiful setup, Hailey's tone shifts from playful annoyance to genuine excitement. "So, what do you think? Is it 'soft launch' worthy?"

Walking over, I take in the details—the assorted cheeses, fresh grapes, and strawberries, thin slices of prosciutto, all perfectly arranged. A bottle of rosé chills in a bucket next to two fluted glasses. I have to admit, the scene is pretty impressive.

"You've outdone yourself," I commend genuinely. "It's like something out of a movie."

Hailey beams, obviously proud of her handiwork. "Just part of the job. Now, are you ready to play your part?"

I salute her mock-seriously, "Always, ma'am."

With a playful shove, she laughs. "Good. Now sit. We have a lot of pretending to do."

Ah, the things I put myself through. But as I settle down next to Hailey, the sun warming our skin, the aroma of the ocean filling the air, and the promise of a delightful charcuterie waiting, I think maybe, just maybe, it won't be so hard to pretend after all.

The air is filled with the soft sound of waves crashing, and a few distant voices from other beachgoers. As I lounge back, my fingers just teasing the edge of the blanket, Hailey gets into full photographer mode. She moves, adjusting angles, considering the light, her face scrunched in concentration. One moment she's capturing the side of my face as I gaze out at the horizon, the next, she's snapping a shot of our intertwined fingers, then our plates, drinks, and everything in between.

Once satisfied, she pulls out her phone to inspect her work. "Okay, check these out," she says, handing the device over to me.

I scroll through. The photos are surprisingly good, cryptic enough to get the internet buzzing. There's one where she's capturing just the bottom half of our faces, our lips inches apart, and it's oddly intimate. Another shows our feet, side by side in the sand, hers adorned with dainty silver anklets. The captions she adds are even more intriguing, peppered with cryptic emojis like the eyes, a heart, and even a ring.

I raise an eyebrow. "I thought you said you weren't good at this social media stuff?"

She grins, waving a dismissive hand. "Oh, I had an emergency meeting with the zoomers this morning. Got a crash course in Instagram aesthetics and emoji language."

I can't help but chuckle. "Impressive. I knew there was a reason I always thought you were smarter than me."

She winks. "That's because I am."

My gaze drops to her hands as she types. "Those nails of yours look incredible, by the way."

She fans her fingers out, admiring the soft pink polish. "Well, since my face isn't going to be in the shots, I have to work with what I've got. Besides, a girl's got to have pretty nails."

"Speaking of shots," I interject, getting up and stretching, "how about some 'playing in the surf' pics? You did say to dress to get wet."

Hailey eyes me, a spark of mischief in her eyes. "Thought you'd never ask."

Before I can process what's happening, she's pulling her shirt over her head, revealing a stunning bikini top that leaves very little to the imagination. I'm momentarily stunned, taking in the sight. She catches me ogling, smirking as she saunters past with a flirtatious sway.

"Enjoying the view, are we?" she teases, her voice dripping with playful sarcasm.

I snap back to reality, clearing my throat. "I, uh, just didn't expect... I mean, wow."

She chuckles, flipping her hair over her shoulder. "Keep your eyes on the prize, Max. We've got pictures to take."

With that, she dashes into the surf, beckoning me to follow. And as the waves crash around us and the camera clicks away, I can't help but think that this fake engagement thing might just turn out to be a lot more real than I'd ever imagined.

17

Hailey

THE SUN HAD LOWERED a bit, painting the sky with hues of pinks and purples that reflected on the water. We're lounging on the beach, our shoes discarded, feet buried in the cool sand. Between us is a bottle of rosé, two half-filled glasses, and a charcuterie board that's about polished off.

I pick up a cube of cheese, trying to be nonchalant, but my other hand is occupied scrolling through the avalanche of notifications on my phone. The reactions are more than I'd hoped for. The internet is on fire.

I can't help but grin, showing Max a particular tweet, "This one says, 'Who's the mystery girl with Max Decker?' followed by like, fifty detective emojis."

Max chuckles, sipping his wine. "Oh, and here's a good one, 'Max Decker has been seen on Cedarwood Beach. Anyone know who the girl is? She better treat our boy right!'" He imitates a stern voice on the last bit, making me laugh.

We clink glasses, triumphant. I watch as the bubbles in my rosé dance, and then take a sip. It's tart, refreshing. Perfect for this moment.

"The internet sleuths are out in full force," Max says, scrolling through his own phone. "Everyone's trying to figure out who you are. Some are even speculating you're a secret childhood sweetheart."

I laugh, almost choking on my wine. "Childhood sweetheart? Oh, that's rich. Although, considering our history, not entirely inaccurate."

His eyes meet mine, a glint of mischief there. "They're not too far off, are they?"

I shake my head. "No, they're not."

We sit in a comfortable silence for a moment, enjoying the sounds of the ocean and the distant laughter of beachgoers. But then an idea hits me. "You know, we could give them a little more to talk about," I say, looking over at Max. "One more pic. Just to... seal the deal."

His eyebrows raise, intrigued. "What did you have in mind?"

I smirk, inching closer. "How about a little PDA?"

He chuckles. "You mean...?"

I nod, biting my lip. "A kiss. One good enough to set social media ablaze."

He grins, leaning in. "You sure?"

I roll my eyes. "It's for the 'gram, remember?"

Our faces are inches apart. The air between us grows thick, charged. And then, without another word, our lips meet. It's soft, sweet, a mere brush, but then it deepens, becoming more intense, more real. And for a moment, I forget why we're doing this in the first place. I forget about the charade, the social media, everything.

Until Max pulls back with a smirk. "Did you get it?"

I blink, reality rushing back. "Oh. Oh! The picture!" My face flushes, embarrassed that I got so lost in the moment.

He chuckles. "Caught up in the moment, were we?"

I give him a playful shove. "Shut up." Then, taking a deep breath, I position the phone once more. "Okay, take two."

This time, I'm ready. And as our lips meet again, I snap the perfect shot. The two of us, silhouetted against the setting sun, lost in a kiss.

Pulling away, I can't help but grin. "Now *that* should do the trick. Like I said, for someone who claimed to be clueless about social media, you're a natural."

I shrug, snuggling into his side. "What can I say? I'm a fast learner."

Sand sticking to my skin, the sound of waves lapping, and the aftertaste of that kiss—everything feels far too comfortable, cozy even. I shake off the feeling, straightening my back with abruptness that would make a drill sergeant proud. *Stay focused, Hailey*, I tell myself.

Taking a deep breath, I grab my phone for another social media scan. Sure enough, our silhouette against the setting sun, locked in a kiss, has rocketed its way through the internet.

"Looks like we've got a trending hashtag," I say, showing Max the screen. "#MysteryKiss."

His eyes crinkle in a pleased smile. "Well, damn. I knew you were the right woman for the job."

"It's all strategic," I reply, trying to maintain an air of professionalism, but that shared smile between us just moments ago keeps replaying in my mind.

"We're on the right track," I say, needing to refocus. "If we continue with this gradual reveal, by the time we drop the engagement ring photo, it'll not just break but utterly *melt* the internet."

He stretches out, his arm brushing mine, and that simple contact sends my heart into a ridiculous flutter. "So, do you want to hang out a bit longer? The sunset's looking particularly beautiful tonight."

There's that charm again. The one that's just so... Max.

I hesitate. The beach, the wine, the setting sun—it's all too tempting. And the man beside me? Dangerous territory. While I'd love nothing more than to spend more time here, my instincts scream otherwise. I've seen too many rom-coms to know how this scene goes.

Clearing my throat, I begin to pack up our things. "You know, I think it's best if I get going. It's been a long day, and we've got a big week ahead."

Max watches me for a moment, a hint of something I can't quite decipher in his eyes. "Right," he says slowly. "Of course."

The air grows a tad more tense, the previous ease fading as I fumble with the blanket, trying to fold it neatly. He stands up, offering a hand to help me. Our fingers brush, and a jolt of something undefinable passes between us. We both pull back, startled.

"All set?" he asks, voice a bit gruffer than usual.

I nod, avoiding his gaze. "Yeah, thanks."

We walk towards the parking lot, the silence between us heavy but not entirely uncomfortable. I keep my gaze firmly on the ground, while he seems lost in thought.

As we reach my car, he turns to face me. "Hailey," he begins, voice soft.

I look up, meeting his eyes. "Yeah?"

He pauses, as if searching for the right words. "Today was... fun. Thanks for being such a good sport about all of this."

I smile, feeling a warmth spread through me. "It's all part of the job," I reply, although I'm not entirely sure I believe that myself.

With a final nod, I open my car door. "See you tomorrow, Max."

And with that, I drive away, leaving behind a sunset, a trending hashtag, and a whole lot of unanswered questions.

***

THE NEXT DAY

The smell of fresh-brewed coffee and the soft chatter of early morning customers is comforting. It's been my refuge for years, and this morning is no different. I sink into the plush armchair opposite Lucy, my fingers wrapped around a steaming mug.

"So?" Lucy probes, her eyes scanning my face with that unnerving best friend's intuition.

"We launched," I confess, biting my lip. "Softly. You know, beach pics, shadowy profiles, and..." I trail off, hesitating.

Lucy raises an eyebrow. "And?"

I groan. "And one very public kiss."

Lucy's eyes widen, but before she can say anything, I hear giggles from the table behind us. There's a group of young women, phones in hand, animatedly discussing something. I lean slightly, trying not to be obvious, and hear snippets.

"...Max is totally seeing someone!"

"...but who's the mystery girl?"

"...OMG, those nails though. They're so freaking cool!"

My gaze flits down to my own nails, painted in a distinctive shade of lilac with a tiny star on each thumb. I glance around nervously, and I swear a girl seated near the window is squinting at my hands, then back at her phone, then back at my hands.

"Lucy," I hiss, "I think she's onto me!"

Lucy rolls her eyes, a smirk playing on her lips. "Oh please, Hailey. You're just being paranoid. Cedarwood's a big town. Lots of women have pretty nails."

"But not *these* nails," I protest weakly, feeling like I've painted targets on my fingertips.

She snorts, taking a sip of her tea. "You're overthinking it."

I pull out my phone, checking our Instagram post from the beach. The comments section is filled with speculation, and my heart leaps into my throat when I see several people mentioning the nails. *Yikes.*

Pulling myself together, I look back at Lucy. "Regardless, the plan's working. People are talking, speculating, guessing. By the time we drop the big news, Cedarwood won't know what hit it."

Lucy sighs, leaning back. "It's not the plan I'm worried about, Hales. It's you. This whole thing is a lie, and we both know how Max can be. What if he breaks your heart again?"

I shake my head, determined. "He won't. I've got it all under control. It's just business, Lucy. Nothing more."

But even as the words leave my mouth, I can feel the weight of that sunset kiss pressing on my mind.

Lucy looks like she wants to argue further but then bites her lip, choosing her words carefully. "I just don't want to see you hurt again, okay?"

"I appreciate that," I say, reaching across the table to squeeze her hand. "But trust me. I know what I'm doing."

Our deep conversation is interrupted by a loud ping from my phone. I glance down, and my heart skips a beat. It's a message from my mom.

Hailey! Why didn't you tell me you're dating Max?!

I choke on my coffee, spluttering and coughing as Lucy pats my back. "Oh my god," I wheeze. "How did she know?"

Lucy snorts, trying not to laugh. "Well, she is on Facebook."

I groan, burying my face in my hands. "This is going to be a long day."

18

Max

THE AMBER GLOW OF the setting sun paints Cedarwood's streets in rich hues of gold and orange. The sight would be calming if it weren't for the knot of dread in my stomach that seems to twist tighter with each step I take. Autumn has never felt this tense.

My phone buzzes, and I quickly pull it out, glancing at the screen. A stream of texts from Jake lights up my notifications.

Dude, what the hell? My sister?

You know you're walking into the lion's den, right?

I mean, even I'm scared of Mom when she's in "mama bear" mode.

I can't help but smirk at that. Jake, a beast of a man himself, scared of his own mother? But I've seen Karen in action; she's no joke.

I type back hurriedly, trying to diffuse the situation:

Calm down, man. It's complicated. We'll talk later, I promise.

There's a short pause, which feels like forever, then Jake's response pops up.

You better. Because if you hurt her, "best friends" won't mean a thing.

I sigh, stopping for a moment to lean against a lamppost. Understood. Talk soon.

I pocket my phone and keep walking. The familiar scent of burning wood wafts from chimneys, and children play on sidewalks, their laughter echoing in the crisp air. A reminder of simpler times.

I reach the end of the street and find myself standing before the house that holds so many memories. It's a beautiful two-story Victorian, adorned with twinkling lights. It's inviting, but it might as well be the gates of Mordor right now.

Deep breath, Max. You've faced down entire teams of giants on the rink, you can handle one dinner.

Summoning all the courage I have, I stride up to the front door and knock. Almost immediately, it swings open to reveal Karen, her brows raised in surprise but a warm smile on her lips.

"Well, if it isn't Max Decker," she says, her voice dripping with mirth. "Come to face the music?"

I chuckle nervously, scratching the back of my neck. "Something like that."

Robert, Hailey's father, appears behind her, giving me a firm nod. "Evening, Max."

"Evening, Mr. Rogers," I reply, maintaining my confident facade, though inside I'm a ball of nerves.

Karen chuckles. "Well, come in then. No use standing out in the cold. We're all eager to hear this story."

Thunder crashes again, echoing like an ominous warning. I instinctively look over my shoulder, catching the sudden onset of dark, churning clouds. The weather had been so clear a moment ago, but now it's as though the universe is reflecting the mood inside this house.

"Looks like quite the storm's brewing," Robert comments, peeking through the sheer curtains. "Wasn't expecting that."

I nod, shaking off the unease. "Neither was I."

My gaze instinctively searches for Hailey and finds her in the kitchen. Even when she's flustered, she manages to look effortlessly adorable. Her hair is pulled up in a messy bun, a few stray tendrils framing her face. She shoots me a glance, her smile shaky, eyes screaming 'Help!'

Robert, always the gracious host despite the tension, offers, "Drink, Max?"

"That'd be great, thanks." Might as well, I think. Liquid courage and all.

As he starts preparing it, I can't help but let curiosity get the better of me. "So, how did you guys even find out? The whole point was to be discreet."

Karen, never one to be outdone, takes out her phone with a triumphant air. She swipes a few times and then turns the screen towards me. It's the intimate shot of our interlocked hands, a symbol of our 'relationship.'

"Well, your little photo shoot was such a hit that it managed to end up on my Facebook feed. You see this?" she says, pointing at a small, barely noticeable birthmark on the inside of Hailey's middle finger. "I'd recognize that anywhere."

Hailey groans, burying her face in her hands. "Mom, seriously?"

Karen continues, unabashed, "When you've changed as many diapers and treated as many boo-boos as I have, you remember every little detail of your baby."

I can't help it; I burst out laughing. The absurdity of the situation, being outed by a birthmark, it's too much. Hailey shoots me a mock glare, but there's a hint of amusement in her eyes.

"Okay, okay, you got us," I concede, holding up my hands in surrender.

Karen smirks, clearly pleased with herself, while Robert hands me the drink, a twinkle of amusement in his eyes.

"Well, now that the cat's out of the bag," Robert begins, "let's sit down and have a proper chat. Takeout's on the way."

A chat? Why does that sound like the most ominous thing ever? I take a deep sip of my drink, bracing myself for the inquisition ahead.

The rich aroma of tacos, enchiladas, and spicy salsa fills the dining room. Karen really outdid herself with the choice of takeout. As we dig into the delicious spread, the table is momentarily filled with the sounds of munching and appreciative hums.

Finally, Robert breaks the silence, pointing a fork at me. "So, what's the story? Why all the secrecy?"

Hailey takes a deep breath, and we exchange a quick glance. We're in this together.

"You see, Dad," Hailey starts, her voice just a hint shaky, "It all began when Max reached out to me a while ago. We started texting, then talking, and before we knew it, hours would go by with us just chatting away."

I jump in, eager to keep the narrative flowing. "It was unexpected, for both of us. I mean, I've known Hailey forever, but this... it was different. We connected on a level that neither of us had ever experienced before."

Hailey nods in agreement. "We didn't want to make a big deal out of it until we were sure of what we had. And with Max's sudden return to Cedarwood, it just felt right to wait a bit, you know, see if what we had long-distance would translate in person."

I can't believe how easily the story is coming together. It's a lie, yes, but a well-constructed one. The two of us, spinning this tale, it's like we're in sync. She takes the shot and I'm the goalie. And vice versa.

Karen, ever the romantic, sighs dreamily. "Oh, that's so sweet. A modern-day love story."

Robert raises an eyebrow but remains silent, clearly letting us finish.

"But, Mom, Dad," Hailey interjects, "we were going to tell you, I promise. We just wanted to do a... what did you call it, Max?"

I chuckle. "A 'soft launch' on social media."

Robert wrinkles his nose. "Soft what now?"

I can't help but grin. "Okay, so it's like when a company rolls out a new product but doesn't make a big announcement. They just kind of... put it out there and see how people react."

Hailey continues, "In our case, we were dropping hints about our relationship without actually confirming anything. Just to see what the response would be. And to build buzz, of course."

Karen tilts her head. "And what's the response been like?"

I clear my throat, trying to suppress a smirk. "Let's just say the internet's in a bit of a frenzy."

Robert and Karen share a look, one that suggests that while they understand, they don't get it. Hard to explain the concept of clout to folks not heavily into social media, I guess.

After the plates are cleared, Robert stands up, gesturing towards his study. "Max, care for an after-dinner drink? I've got a new whiskey I'd like you to try."

I raise an eyebrow, a little surprised. "Lead the way," I reply, trying to keep my cool.

The study is dimly lit with a warm amber hue, a reflection of the vintage mahogany furnishings. Bottles line the shelves, from floor to ceiling, some with names I recognize and others that look more exotic.

Robert pours two glasses of a deep, amber liquid. "This is a 25-year-old single malt. Thought we'd break it out for a special occasion."

As the liquid touches my lips, its smoky aroma engulfs me. It's smooth, rich, with a hint of peat. The warmth runs down my throat, giving me a slight comfort in the slightly tense atmosphere.

Robert sips his drink, then leans back, surveying me with those piercing eyes. "Max," he begins, "I've heard a lot about you, especially from the years you were away. And not all of it has been... flattering."

I take another sip, waiting for what's to come next.

"I don't want to sound like a cliché," he continues, "but Haile y... she's my world. And the last thing I want is for her to be with someone who might not treat her with the respect she deserves. I hope I'm making myself clear."

I nod. "Perfectly."

The weight of the moment bears down on me, but I face him squarely. "Look, Mr. Rogers, I won't lie. I've made mistakes in the past, who hasn't? But what Hailey and I have... it's real. And I intend to treat her with nothing but the utmost respect. She's in good hands, I promise."

Robert stares at me for a moment longer, then nods slowly, taking another sip from his glass. "Good to hear."

With that, our chat comes to a close. I'm relieved, to be honest. Facing a father's scrutiny is no easy task.

I head downstairs, eager to escape the intensity of the study. Hailey and Karen are chatting in the kitchen, and I offer to help clean up.

"Let me take out the recycling," I suggest, gathering up the empty wine and whiskey bottles.

Hailey chuckles. "Always the gentleman, huh?"

I wink at her. "Just doing my part."

As I step outside, I'm greeted by a sudden, sharp gust of wind. And before I can react, the skies open up, drenching me with rain in mere seconds. My shirt clings to me, and my hair is dripping wet.

I rush back inside, bottles in hand, to the sound of Hailey's laughter.

"You look like a drowned rat," she teases.

"Charming," I retort, wringing out my hair. "Note to self: always check the weather forecast."

Karen rushes over with an urgency that surprises me, thrusting a thick towel into my hands. "Oh dear, you're absolutely drenched!" she exclaims.

"I hadn't noticed," I quip, flashing her my best smirk. But the shiver that runs through me gives me away.

Karen clucks her tongue, shaking her head. "Come with me. You can't stay in those wet clothes. Robert has some loungewear you can borrow."

I follow her up the grand staircase, slightly apprehensive about wearing another man's clothes. As we enter what appears to be a walk-in closet the size of my first apartment, Karen rummages around, pulling out a pair of soft-looking joggers and a loose-fitting tee.

"This should do the trick," she says, handing them to me. "Go ahead and change in the guest room next door."

I nod gratefully, disappearing to change. And let me tell you, there's nothing quite like the feeling of dry, soft fabric against your skin after a surprise rain shower. Refreshed, I head back downstairs, finding Hailey trying and failing to suppress a giggle.

"Looking cozy," she teases.

"Feeling it," I retort, doing a quick twirl to show off my borrowed threads.

But the storm outside only seems to be getting worse, with the wind howling and rain lashing against the windows.

Karen looks at me, concern evident in her eyes. "You can't possibly leave in this weather, Max. It's not safe. You'll have to stay the night."

I'm about to politely decline when Hailey jumps in. "Mom's right. It's too dangerous out there."

I'm caught off guard by the intensity of her gaze, and the unspoken message behind her words. Are we really going to be sharing a bed tonight?

19

Hailey

My childhood room is a time capsule. Max seems to get a kick out of the collage of band posters, angsty song lyrics scrawled across notepaper, and polaroid pictures strewn about. I watch as his eyes scan the walls, a smirk dancing on his lips.

"You were a One Direction fan?" he teases, pointing at a poster of the boys in their prime.

I scoff, feigning annoyance. "Aren't we all Directioners deep down?" I say with faux solemnity. "Though I've grown up, some treasures are just too hard to part with."

He chuckles. "I'll let you have that one. But, uh, Twilight? Really?"

My cheeks flare, and I give a mock glare. "Hey! Edward Cullen was dreamy."

"Was?" Max arches an eyebrow.

"Okay, fine. He still is," I grumble, but I can't help the laugh that escapes me.

The atmosphere shifts slightly as Max sits on the edge of my bed, the weight of our earlier conversation returning. "Look, Hailey," he begins, his tone more serious, "I know today was... a lot. Lying to your parents and all."

I sigh, biting my lip. "I just hate not being honest with them. Especially over something like this."

He nods, understandingly. "But remember, this is for a good cause. We're helping them save the house. And besides," he offers with a shrug, "it's not like we're doing anything too wrong. We're just... bending the truth a little."

I raise an eyebrow, a little surprised. "Max, are you... being empathetic right now?"

He chuckles, scratching the back of his neck. "Even us jocks have feelings, you know. I get it. Family's important. And sometimes, it's hard to keep things from them."

I nod, taking in his words. "I just hope we're making the right call."

"We are," he says confidently. "And soon enough, everything will be out in the open, and they'll be none the wiser. Promise."

There's a moment of quiet understanding between us, and for the first time, I truly appreciate the depth beneath Max's playful exterior. As the storm continues to howl outside, I find unexpected comfort in his presence.

"Thanks," I murmur, "for understanding."

The rhythmic patter of raindrops against the window creates an oddly soothing backdrop. Beside me, Max sits with a quiet, thoughtful expression that I've never quite seen on him before. It's unsettling, mostly because I don't want to get used to this version of Max. It's dangerously easy to forget our history when he's being empathetic and surprisingly... human.

It's a dangerous game I'm playing with my own heart. Deep down, the sting of our past still throbs. The betrayal, the hurt, the confusion... none of it has been fully resolved. Max may have grown up, but he's never once approached the topic of the gaping wound he left in my teenage heart. How can I trust him now when he hasn't even acknowledged the past?

My train of thought is interrupted when Max clears his throat, shattering the silence. "So, uh, about our sleeping arrangements," he begins, running a hand through his hair. His attempt at casualness would've been comical if I wasn't so preoccupied with our complicated emotional dance.

I raise an eyebrow, waiting.

"Look, I get that it'd be weird if I bunk in a guest room, considering our 'relationship' and all," he says, using air quotes. "But I can take the floor if that's what you prefer."

I can't help but scoff at his gallant offer. "Please, it's not 1923. We're adults. We can share a bed without it being a thing," I retort, trying to hide the nervous flutter in my stomach.

Max's smirk returns. "Didn't know if you were ready for the wild experience of sleeping beside the Max Decker."

Rolling my eyes, I shoot back, "Oh, trust me. I'm sure it'll be riveting. Just don't snore."

His chuckle is genuine. "No promises."

The soft rustle of sheets fills the room as we both adjust, trying to find a comfortable position. Max's voice breaks the silence, dripping with faux seriousness. "Just wondering—should I keep an eye out for your Harry Potter nightlight? Y'know, to ward off any potential dementors?"

I snort, hiding my face in my pillow to stifle my giggles. "Oh, shut up. It's not a nightlight; it's a Lumos charm."

He chuckles, and I'm reminded once more of how weirdly easy this all feels, how strangely familiar his presence beside me is. I had sworn to keep my distance, to protect my heart, but his humor has a way of breaking down my defenses.

Shaking my head, I roll away from him, facing the opposite direction. The weight of the past and the thrill of the present mingles in my head. It's surreal. A decade ago, teenage Hailey would have been swooning at the mere thought of sharing a room with Max Decker. The heartthrob. The rebel. And yet, here we are, decades later, mere inches apart under the same blanket.

Caught in my thoughts, a sudden warmth rushes through me. Embarrassed by the unexpected surge of desire, I mentally scold myself. 'You have to keep it together, Hailey.'

Suddenly, the mattress shifts and I can feel Max stretching, his long frame pressing against the bed. He's sprawling, like he's the king of this domain and I'm just his very annoyed roommate.

I whip around to shoot him a playful glare for hogging the bed, but the words die in my throat. The soft glow from the street-lights filters through the curtains, casting a gentle illumination on his face. He's close. Very close. Our gazes lock, the air around us growing thick with tension. His stormy blue eyes, usually so playful and carefree, are now serious and probing.

Time seems to slow, every heartbeat echoing loudly in the silence of the room. For a split second, everything else—the fake relationship, the past hurt, the stakes at hand—fades away. All that remains is the two of us, locked in this intimate, electrifying moment.

"I, uh..." I stammer, searching for words but coming up empty. The moment hangs between us, charged and intense.

He swallows hard, the slightest hint of a smile playing on his lips. "You were saying?"

The raw energy between us is undeniable. Like two opposing magnets being drawn together, it feels inevitable and impossible to resist. Inch by inch, the scant distance between us shrinks. I can hear the rhythmic beat of my own heart, pounding loudly against the cage of my chest.

'No, Hailey,' I scold myself internally. 'Remember the plan. Remember the rules. Remember everything.' But the louder my mind protests, the more tempting his presence becomes. It's as if all the unresolved feelings from the past are demanding their due.

It's so, so wrong, and yet, as our lips meet, everything feels right. The world narrows down to the sensation of his mouth on mine. Every nerve ending tingles, every thought evaporates. The rain pounds against the windowpane, punctuating the moment, amplifying the intensity. His lips are warm, soft, yet insistent, and they pull me in deeper than I anticipated.

My head is spinning, drowning in the torrent of sensations, and emotions that I'd tucked away come flooding back. His taste is intoxicating. The sensation of him—the mix of strength and gentleness—sets my entire body alight. Before I realize it, his hand begins to slide up my shirt, each touch sending a shiver down my spine.

It's at this precise moment, as the storm outside mirrors the one inside, that a lightning bolt of clarity strikes me. With a gasp, I break away, our foreheads still touching. Both of us are breathless, eyes wide and searching, processing what just transpired.

"Hailey..." he begins, his voice rough with need and surprise.

I shake my head, attempting to clear the haze of desire. "Max... we can't."

He pulls back slightly, giving us both space to breathe. "I know," he murmurs, running a hand through his drenched hair. "But damn, Hailey... that was..."

"Unexpected?" I suggest, my voice quivering.

He chuckles softly, the tension easing just a bit. "That's one way to put it."

We both take a moment, letting the rain's rhythmic patter serve as a soothing backdrop. Despite the physical distance we've placed between ourselves, there's an undeniable connection lingering in the air.

There's a playful smirk playing on Max's lips, and those piercing blue eyes of his are studying me with a hint of amusement and wonder.

"Look, Hailey," he starts, his voice dropping to that velvety tone that's hard to resist, "We don't have to... you know. We can just sleep."

But my body has other ideas. Every nerve ending is alive, every sensation heightened. My rational mind may have been trying to keep me on track before, but now, the desire coursing through me is too powerful to deny.

"Screw it," I declare, almost defiantly. Grabbing his face, I pull him into a searing kiss. I've always been the kind of person to think things through, to weigh pros and cons, but in this moment, overthinking is the enemy. All I want is to lose myself in him.

The taste of him is addictive, his response instantaneous. His hands, warm and firm, roam freely, mapping the contours of my body. The sensation sends sparks flying across my skin. I impatiently tug at his sweater, wanting to feel more of him, and he gets the message loud and clear. In one swift motion, it's discarded, leaving his chiseled torso exposed to my eager hands.

He breaks the kiss momentarily, leaning back and looking down at me with those deep-set, intense eyes. His grin is infectious, a mix of mischief and desire. "You know, Hailey," he starts, trailing one finger slowly from the base of my neck down to my waist, "I never really understood the term 'fine wine' until I met you."

I roll my eyes, trying to suppress a smile. "Are you saying I've aged?"

He laughs, deep and throaty. "Only to perfection," he purrs, pressing gentle kisses along my collarbone.

I feel a tinge of insecurity, remembering the last time we were this close. The young body I once took for granted has changed over the years. The curve of my hips is fuller, the softness around my waist more pronounced. I can't help but wonder if he notices, if he minds.

Max seems to sense my hesitance. Drawing back, he cups my face, locking his gaze with mine. "Hey," he says softly. "Every line, every mark, every change? It tells a story. And to me, it's the most beautiful one."

His fingers trace the curve of my waist, his touch feather-light. "This," he breathes against my neck, "is the curve that drives me wild."

I can't help the giggle that escapes my lips. "You're just saying that."

He smirks. "Want me to prove it?"

A shiver courses through me at the promise in his voice. As his lips find mine again, my worries evaporate. With Max, I feel celebrated, desired, cherished.

Max's touches are both skillful and insistent. He knows just where to press, where to linger, sending wave after wave of pleasure crashing through me. I lose myself in the sensations, in the rise and fall of our breathing, the raw, unspoken promises exchanged between heated glances.

He reaches down, slipping his hand underneath my panties. I'm already soaking wet, ready for more. Max kisses me hard, spreading my lips and teasing me with expert precision, making me yearn as he moves closer and closer to my clit. A small smile forms on his mouth, and I get the sense he knows just how crazy he's making me.

I moan, and he finally touches me right where I want him. The pleasure is instantaneous, his fingertip making slow circles around my clit, the intensity building and building. I buck my hips against him, yearning for more with my body.

By the time he finally spreads me open and enters me, I'm done. He keeps the pressure with his thumb on my clit, and the twin sensations of him inside of me and on my most sensitive place make me lose my mind. I open my mouth, ready to scream. His hand shoots to my mouth, covering me up, reminding me that I'm most definitely in a place where I don't want to make any noise.

I come hard, and when I'm done, I'm a panting mess, my head resting on his round, broad shoulder.

And I'm ready for much, much more.

20

Max

THERE'S A LIGHTNESS IN my chest as I lay beside Hailey, feeling the warmth of our closeness. I've been with many women, but there's something distinct about the way Hailey moves, the way she breathes, the way her eyes darken with desire. It's intoxicating.

I can't shake the image of her, lost in pleasure, from my mind. It's a sight that would make angels weep, or devils cheer—probably both. And now, as we kiss, there's a fire between us that's only grown fiercer.

"Come here," she says.

"I am here."

"No—even closer." She grins. "I was thinking about what you said before, about you getting to taste me."

I grin. "Is that right?"

"Yep. And... made me realize that I didn't have the pleasure either."

"No time like the present."

"You're on the money about that."

Her kisses are soft and searching, exploring every inch of my mouth as if it's new territory. I let out a low groan as her fingers trail down, teasing over my abs, then moving lower. She stops over the waistband of my sweatpants, her touch electric, and for a moment, I think she's going to retreat. But then her hand dives beneath, and I lose all coherent thought.

There's a twinkle in her eye as she gauges my reaction, a hint of mischief that makes my heart race even faster. My world narrows to the sensation of her hands on me, skillful and certain. Then, she takes things up a notch, shifting so that her lips replace her hand. She starts with slow licks along the length of my shaft, sucking on my balls for a few sweet seconds before opening her mouth and taking me inside.

I prop myself up on my elbows, watching as she devotes herself to the task, the way her lips move, the warmth of her breath, the sharp flick of her tongue against me, the wicked gleam in her eyes every time she catches my gaze. My grip tightens on the sheets, every nerve ending screaming with anticipation. She's good, so damn good, and she knows it.

"Hailey," I gasp out, feeling that familiar tightening coil, that delicious precipice of release.

She only hums in response, the vibration sending another jolt of pleasure through me. It's a race now, a battle of wills. I want to hold out, to savor every second, but she's relentless, pushing, teasing, bringing me right to the edge, then back, then to the edge again.

Finally, I can't hold back any longer. "I'm close," I warn her, and she only doubles her efforts, taking me over the edge with an intensity that leaves me breathless and shaking.

With all the restraint I have, I guide her off me, my manhood glistening as she removes her mouth.

"Seemed like you enjoyed that," she says, a devilish little grin on her lips.

"Almost too much," I say. "Nearly finished me."

"And what'd be wrong with that? I *did* say I wanted to taste you, after all."

God, the idea of her making me come with her mouth, watching her drink down every last drop... it's enough to make me want her to go right back to work. But a glance down between her legs reminds me that I'm not nearly done with her yet. With a smooth, effortless motion, I wrap my arm around her waist and move her onto her back.

She gasps, her eyes wide and her mouth a perfect *O* of surprise. I grab her legs and she wraps them around me, wordlessly guiding my hardness towards her. She gasps as I graze her entrance with my cock, and with one more kiss, I sink into her.

My breath comes fast and uneven as I feel her warmth surround me. It's electrifying, every movement between us amplified a thousand times. The sensation of being connected, of becoming one with another person, especially someone like Hailey, is hard to put into words.

With each thrust, I can feel the world fading away. The storm outside, the scheme we concocted, all of it dissolves into the background as we chase pleasure together. The sounds she makes, her breathless moans, the way she clutches at me, pulling me closer—it's a dance, an age-old rhythm of two people losing themselves in one another.

I expected this to be a fun, no-strings-attached fling, something to pass the time and maybe settle a score or two. But this? This feels... different. Deeper. More intimate than I'd bargained for.

Our pace quickens, and with each push and pull, I feel myself getting closer and closer to that edge. And from the way Hailey's breathing changes, the way her grip tightens, I can tell she's right there with me. With one final, shared shudder, we're both tumbling over that precipice, pleasure washing over us in waves.

The storm outside seems to calm as we lay there, spent and satisfied. Hailey curls into me, resting her head on my chest, and I can feel her heart racing beneath my hand. My fingers trace lazy patterns on her back, enjoying the feeling of her soft skin under my touch.

I never thought it would be like this. Never thought it'd be so... connected. In the past, it was always about the chase, the thrill of the conquest. But with Hailey, it's different. There's an intimacy, a depth of connection I've never felt before. And it scares the hell out of me.

I mean, I'm Max Decker. The man who never settles, who never commits. The guy who's built his whole life on fleeting moments and surface-level relationships. And yet, here I am, holding a woman close, feeling something I can't quite put my finger on.

It's too quiet. I need to say something, do something. So, in typical Max fashion, I crack a joke. "So... bet you didn't see this coming when you had those band posters on your wall."

She chuckles, the sound warm and content. "You're such a goof. But no, definitely didn't see this one coming."

"I'm glad it did," I admit, surprised at my own honesty. "Tonight was... unexpected. In the best possible way."

She tilts her head up to look at me, and there's a softness, a vulnerability in her eyes that I've never seen before. "Yeah," she whispers, "it really was."

As we drift off to sleep, wrapped up in each other's arms, I can't shake the feeling that something has shifted between us. And as unsettling as it is, I can't help but hope it leads us somewhere good.

***

The next morning brings a disconcerting cocktail of emotions. The warmth of Hailey's body against mine feels divine. But as reality and the memories of last night set in, the awkwardness is palpable. The cold morning light has a way of making everything seem more exposed. I glance over to see her eyes flutter open, and there's a brief moment of sheer panic in her expression before it settles into something more neutral.

We're both naked, and the sheets are tangled around us. It's almost comical, like something out of a cheesy rom-com, but without the convenient cutaway scene. I've always been a fan of the morning after, but this... this is uncharted territory.

There's this tension in the room, an uncertainty hanging in the air. And, as always, when in doubt, I resort to humor.

"Morning," I say, stretching out in an exaggerated manner, "Nice to see you decided to stick around for the sequel." I gesture down at our disheveled state.

Her face twists, not in the amused smirk I'm expecting but into a frown. "Really, Max?" she snaps, "Is that what this is to you? A joke?"

"Hey, I just—" I start, but she's already moving, pulling the sheets around her as she gets out of bed, looking for her clothes.

The lightheartedness I had hoped for evaporates in an instant. My comment, meant to ease the tension, has just amplified it.

"I thought..." She starts, grabbing her shirt from the floor and pulling it on. "I don't know what I thought." She avoids eye contact, busying herself with dressing.

"Hailey, wait," I try, but it's like every word is a step in the wrong direction.

"You just can't help yourself, can you?" she retorts, now pulling on her pants. "You have to make everything a joke."

My stomach twists, realizing the weight of my mistake. "Look, I didn't mean—"

"You never do," she cuts in, zipping up her jeans and shooting me a glare. "You never think before you speak."

It stings because she's right. My mouth often works faster than my brain, especially when I'm nervous or out of my comfort zone. And right now? I'm miles away from my comfort zone.

I pull on my sweatpants and reach out, trying to salvage the situation. "Hailey, please," I say, grabbing her arm gently.

She pulls away. "Just... let me go, okay? We'll talk about this later." She's almost to the door, looking every bit as determined to get away from me as I am to keep her here.

I'm left standing there, a sinking feeling in my chest. I've been in countless beds, had countless mornings after. But this? This feels different. Because, for the first time, I actually care about the person walking away.

I slump onto the bed, running my hands through my hair. What the hell did I just do?

I step out of the room to find my freshly washed and folded clothes resting outside the door. I can't help but smile at the sheer domesticity of it. Karen's motherly touch is evident, and there's a slight pang in my chest. Growing up in foster homes, I never really had someone care enough to do little things like this. I'm used to doing everything on my own. The unexpected gesture hits me in a place I've guarded for years.

Tugging on my regular jeans and t-shirt, I head downstairs, the scent of freshly brewed coffee guiding me. I'm met with the sight of Karen and Robert at the kitchen island, going about their morning routine. They offer warm greetings, but I can't help but notice the elephant in the room—or rather, the lack of one.

Hailey sits at the far end, engrossed in her phone, her body language screaming 'do not approach.' It's obvious she's been discussing our previous evening's escapade with someone—her best friend, perhaps? I mentally kick myself for the way I've let things play out.

Taking a seat across from her, I greet Robert and Karen, exchanging pleasantries and taking a sip of the strong coffee they've made.

The breakfast spread is generous—eggs, bacon, bread and butter. But despite the delightful aroma and my rumbling stomach, all I can think about is the frosty atmosphere emanating from Hailey. We eat and make light conversation, and for a moment, I can pretend there's nothing wrong.

When Robert and Karen excuse themselves, however, it's a different story.

Deciding to be brave, I clear my throat, "Listen, about last night—"

She cuts me off, not even looking up from her phone. "Don't. Let's just... not talk about it, okay?" Her tone is professional, almost business-like.

I frown, taken aback by her abruptness. "Hailey, I'm sorry—"

She sighs, finally locking eyes with me. "Look, Max, I don't want to get into it. Let's just move forward and focus on why we're here. We need to be professional."

It's a punch to the gut. This isn't the warm, fun-loving Hailey I've come to know. It's a version of her that's guarded, hurt, and disappointed. And it's all because of me.

"We've got a lot of work ahead of us over the next month or so," she continues, shifting the topic. "We need to make sure everything's perfect. This has to work."

I nod, feeling like a deflated balloon. "Yeah, you're right."

She checks her watch, and with a last bite of toast, stands up. "We should head onto the town. Make some appearances."

I want to argue, to make her see that I genuinely regret my earlier words. But seeing the determined look on her face, I decide to back off, at least for now. "Alright," I reply, "Let's go."

As we head out, the weight of what's at stake presses down on me. Between saving her parent's home and mending our tattered relationship, the evening ahead is going to be one for the books. I just hope I don't screw it up any further.

21

Hailey

THE CEDARWOOD TAVERN, USUALLY a bustling hub of small-town chatter, is unusually quiet tonight. The mellow tunes from the jukebox meld with the clink of glasses and the occasional laugh from a regular at the bar. It's the perfect backdrop for unwinding after a day that's left my nerves frayed and my patience threadbare, thanks to Max.

I let out a sigh, resting my elbows on the bar and cradling my head in my hands.

"You have no idea, Jake. He's... he's just so infuriating." I pause, biting the inside of my cheek. Part of me aches to spill the truth about the fake engagement, to unload this burden and share it with my brother. But I know I can't risk it. Jake, bless him, has never been great at keeping secrets. His heart's in the right place, but he's a bit of a blabbermouth, and this isn't just my secret to tell.

It's a dance, balancing on the thin line between honesty and necessity. Keeping this from Jake feels like a betrayal, yet I remind myself it's for a greater good. I love my brother, trust him with my life, but this...

this is too delicate, too risky. I can't let my personal feelings jeopardize everything we're working towards.

"Hockey star giving you a rough go of it?" he asks.

So, with a heavy heart, I plaster on a forced smile. "Just the usual Max antics, you know? Never a dull moment with him." My voice is light, but there's a weight in my chest, an unspoken apology for the lie I'm forced to maintain.

Jake pauses, leaning in with an expression that's equal parts concern and curiosity. "What's he done now?"

I can't help but roll my eyes, the events of the day replaying in my mind. "He turns everything into a joke, Jake. Today, we were supposed to discuss the guest list for the engagement party. And do you know what he does? He starts adding fictional characters and celebrities to the list, laughing like it's the funniest thing in the world."

Jake chuckles, but there's a hint of empathy in his eyes. "That does sound like Max. But come on, Hailey, you knew what you were getting into with him. He's always been a joker, even back in high school."

I know Jake's right, but that doesn't quell the frustration simmering inside me. "I know, I know. But it's different when you're doing something this important. I just wish he'd take things more seriously, even for a second."

Jake smirks, an expression that suggests he knows exactly what I'm talking about. It's a look that makes me push for more.

"Come on, Jake, you've known him forever. Why is he like this?"

Leaning back, Jake's face takes on a thoughtful expression. "Max? Oh, he's always been like that, ever since we were kids. Guy's a natural at not taking anything seriously."

"Just in his Decker DNA, huh?" I quip, trying to keep the conversation light despite the growing curiosity inside me.

He gives a half-shrug, a hint of something deeper in his eyes. "Maybe a bit. But there's more to it. He left Cedarwood one day, then showed back up like that, all cocky and closed off." Jake pauses, and I lean in, sensing something important. "You ask me, it's got a lot to do with what happened to his parents."

"His parents? What happened to them?" The question slips out, driven by a sudden urgency to understand Max better.

Jake's expression shifts, a shadow of sorrow passing over his features. "You never heard about it?" He considers his words. "No, of course you didn't—dude was a master of keeping secrets ever since he was a kid. It's a sad story, really. They died in a car accident when he was little. We were all practically in diapers back then."

I blink, processing this. "I don't remember any of that."

"Yeah, well, it happened way before we started school," Jake explains. "Max left Cedarwood when he was barely walking. Got shuttled around different foster homes until they finally found one back here in his hometown."

I'm taken aback, a mix of shock and sympathy washing over me. "I had no idea," I say.

Jake nods, a hint of reluctance in his eyes. "That's intentional. Max doesn't exactly broadcast that part of his life. In fact," he hesitates, "I've probably said too much already."

I open my mouth to ask more, but at that moment, a large party walks into the bar, pulling Jake's attention away. "Gotta go. Duty calls," he says, offering me a small, apologetic smile before heading off to greet the new arrivals.

Left alone with my thoughts, I'm reeling. This new information about Max paints him in an entirely different light. The cocky, carefree facade he's always projected suddenly feels like just that—a facade. It makes me question everything I thought I knew about Max Decker.

22

Max

I'M LEANING AGAINST THE cool glass at the local rec plex, a place that feels more like home than anywhere else in Cedarwood. The rink's alive with the sound of skates against ice and the echo of laughter. Kids whirl around in a free-skate, their parents cheering from the sidelines. It's a scene straight out of my childhood, and nostalgia grips me hard.

I used to spend every spare moment here, dreaming of the NHL, dreaming of escaping the reality of foster homes and the pain of losing my parents. The rink was my sanctuary, a place where I could forget everything and just... skate. It's ironic how life circles back.

Now, with my suspension hanging over me like a dark cloud, I find myself retreating here, seeking solace in the memories. Watching these kids, full of hope and ambition, I can't help but think about Hailey, about how I've been with her. I've been a jerk, using humor to shield myself from showing any real emotion, from showing her... me.

I feel a pang of regret for the way I joked about our last time together. It was meant to be light-hearted, to keep things casual. But the truth is, I'm terrified. Terrified of getting too close, of letting her see the real me, the one who's not always so confident and carefree. The one who still grieves his parents and struggles with the fear of being abandoned again.

And then there's my career. The thought of never stepping onto the ice again for a real game sends a shiver through me colder than any winter. Hockey's been my life, my identity. Without it, who am I? Just Max Decker, the guy who couldn't keep his act together.

The laughter of the kids brings me back to the present. I watch them, so unburdened, and I envy them. They don't know how quickly everything can change, how fast dreams can be derailed.

I should talk to Hailey, explain things. But the words feel like boulders in my throat, heavy and immovable. I'm Max Decker, the guy who never shows weakness, who never lets anyone in. How do I start now? How do I tell her that beneath this facade, I sometimes feel like a scared kid, afraid of losing everything again?

I push off from the glass, feeling the weight of my own thoughts. I need to clear my head, maybe take a few laps around the rink. As I step onto the ice, the familiar chill brings a small sense of relief. Here, at least, I know who I am. Here, I can just be the hockey player, not the guy whose life is teetering on the edge of uncertainty.

As I skate, the air cool against my face, I know I need to find a way to open up to Hailey. I owe her that much. But the fear, the fear of hurting her, of letting her down, it's paralyzing.

Gliding across the ice, I can't help but let a big grin split my face. It's like I'm shedding all the tension, the worries, the reality of my messed-up life for a while. Here, I'm just Max on ice, nothing more, nothing less.

As I round another corner, a group of kids catches my eye. They're probably around 10 or 11, skating with the kind of freedom that only comes with youth. But there's one kid lagging behind, his skates wobbling unsteadily beneath him. Every few seconds, he takes a tumble, and his friends skate on ahead, laughter trailing behind them.

I slow down, approaching the kid who's picking himself up off the ice again. He's got determination in his eyes, even as he tries to brush off the snow from his pants.

"Hey there," I call out, skating up beside him. "You doing okay?"

He looks up, and I'm met with a pair of bright, defiant eyes. "What's it look like? Training for the next Olympic face-planting event," he retorts, his tone a mix of frustration and biting sarcasm.

I chuckle, recognizing a bit of myself in his attitude. "You're not doing too bad, actually. Falling is part of the process."

His eyes widen as he takes a second look at me, recognition dawning. "Wait, you're Max Decker!"

"Guilty as charged," I say with a wink. "Want a few tips to get you up to speed with your friends?"

His face lights up with an eager nod. "Hell yeah!"

We spend the next few minutes working on the basics. I show him how to balance his weight, how to glide smoothly, and how to turn without kissing the ice. The kid's a quick learner; he's got the grit, just lacks the technique.

Soon enough, he's doing laps, not as fast as his friends, but he's definitely keeping up. There's a proud glint in his eye each time he passes me, and it reminds me of the first time I felt like I was flying on the ice.

As I watch the group of friends laughing and racing each other, a thought of Hailey sneaks into my mind. I wonder what she'd think of this moment, of me teaching a kid how to skate. Would it surprise her to see this side of me? The side that isn't all about jokes and cockiness, but about helping a kid find his feet – or skates, in this case.

Hailey's been on my mind a lot lately, especially after our last awkward morning. I wish I could let her see this side of me more often, the side that isn't afraid to be real, to be vulnerable. But I've spent so long building up walls, playing the part of the carefree jock, that I'm not sure how to start breaking them down.

The laughter of the kids echoes around the rink, and I take a deep breath, feeling a strange sense of peace. Maybe, just maybe, I can find a way to show Hailey this part of me. The real me, not just the NHL star or the small-town legend, but the guy who finds joy in simple moments like these.

I take one last look at the kids, their faces red with cold and excitement, and push off the boards, back into my own thoughts. It's time to think about how to be more open with Hailey, to let her in on who I really am. It's a daunting thought, but as I pick up speed, feeling the chill air against my face, I know it's a risk I need to take.

23

Hailey

As we pull up to the yoga studio, my heart races with a blend of excitement and nerves. Max looks at me, his eyebrow cocked in that signature Decker way.

"Ready to turn me into a yoga master?" he teases, but I can tell he's just as anxious.

"Yoga is more than just physical," I start, trying to sound wise. "It's about finding balance, inside and out. It's kind of my haven." I glance at him, hoping he'll understand the depth of what I'm sharing.

Max nods. "Well, then, lead the way, Yogi Hailey."

The studio is a sanctuary of tranquility, with soft, ambient lighting and the gentle hum of a meditative soundtrack. The aroma of lavender and sandalwood fills the air. I breathe in deeply, feeling at home.

Max, on the other hand, looks totally out of place. His gaze flits around the room, taking in the yoga mats, the serene faces of regulars, and the calming décor. Despite his discomfort, there's a willingness in his posture, an openness to try something new.

Our instructor, a lithe figure with a welcoming smile, approaches us. Her eyes widen slightly as she recognizes Max. "It's a pleasure to have you join us, Max. I'm Maya." Her enthusiasm is palpable.

Max shakes her hand, a sheepish grin on his face. "Thanks, Maya. I'm a rookie, so go easy on me."

Maya laughs, her eyes twinkling. "Yoga is a journey, not a competition. Let's find your mat."

The class starts with basic poses—downward dog, warrior, and tree pose. I move into each position with ease, feeling the familiar stretch and balance. Max, however, fumbles through the movements. His warrior pose looks more like a confused soldier, and his tree pose resembles a wilting branch.

I can't help but chuckle at the sight. "You're doing great," I encourage, though it's hard to keep a straight face.

Max shoots me a mock-glare. "I think this yoga thing is rigged against guys like me," he jokes, trying to adjust his stance.

Our banter continues, light and easy, as we move through the poses. Max's attempts bring a few more laughs from me, and even from the instructor. It's heartwarming to see him not take himself too seriously, a side of him I'm starting to appreciate more.

As we transition into a paired pose, Max and I face each other, trying to synchronize our movements. It's a challenge, with Max's awkwardness and my attempts to guide him. Our hands meet, our eyes lock, and for a moment, there's an electric charge in the air, a connection that goes beyond the physicality of the pose.

It's then that I remember the purpose of this outing—to capture some candid shots for social media. I nod towards my phone resting on a nearby shelf. "Let's get some pictures for the 'gram. This is gold."

Max grins, his earlier hesitation replaced by a newfound enthusiasm. "Let's show them how it's done."

We pose, Max attempting another warrior pose while I balance in a tree pose next to him. The result is a comical yet endearing photo that perfectly captures the essence of our outing—fun, a bit messy, but genuine in its own way.

Max, ever the competitor, decides to take on some of the more complex poses. "How hard can it be?" he says with typical bravado. His first attempt at the crow pose ends with a soft thud as he lands on the mat.

I stifle a laugh. "You okay there?" I ask, trying to sound concerned, but the amusement is clear in my voice.

"I've had harder falls on the ice," he grins, getting back up. His next try at the pose is slightly more successful, but his arms wobble, and his concentration is comical.

I find myself watching him, not just with amusement, but with a growing sense of admiration. Max might be out of his element, but he's giving it his all. His usual cockiness is replaced with a genuine effort to keep up, and it's surprisingly endearing.

Maya suggests some partner poses, and Max and I are soon entwined in a series of balances and stretches that require close contact. As I press my back against his chest in a double tree pose, I can feel the warmth of his body, the steady rhythm of his breath. Our arms reach up together, fingers entwined. The pose is intimate, and a surge of heat runs through me, leaving me slightly breathless.

Max's hand brushes against my side as we move into another pose, and I feel a jolt of electricity. The proximity, the touch—it's all starting to blur the lines between our fake relationship and something that feels dangerously real. I try to focus on my breathing, on the pose, but it's a struggle.

We break to take more photos, capturing the hilarity and closeness of the class. Max poses in an exaggerated warrior stance, his face a picture of mock-seriousness. I join him for a photo, our smiles genuine, the chemistry between us palpable even through the lens. The paired pose captures us in a moment of harmony, looking every bit the perfect couple.

Scrolling through the photos, I'm struck by the bittersweet reality. Here we are, looking like a couple deeply in love, yet it's all for show. The laughter, the touches, the shared looks—it's part of our agreement, a charade for the world. Yet, I can't deny the flutter in my stomach, the warmth in my chest. For a moment, I allow myself to imagine what it would be like if this were real, if the man beside me was really mine.

As the class winds down, we settle into a quiet moment of meditation. Max is lying next to me, his breath steady and calm. I glance over at him, watching the rise and fall of his chest. He seems peaceful, a stark contrast to his usual high-energy demeanor.

"You know," he whispers, eyes still closed, "this is a lot different from sprinting down the ice or dodging fists."

I suppress a giggle. "Quieter and less bruising, I imagine."

"Definitely less bruising," he agrees, cracking one eye open to look at me. "But there's something... nice about it. Calming."

It's a side of Max I haven't seen much of, one that's introspective and gentle. It's easy to forget, amid his jokes and bravado, that there's depth to him.

"I'm glad you're finding your zen zone," I reply softly, feeling a warmth spreading through me.

We lie there in silence for a moment, the sounds of the yoga studio—the soft music, the gentle hum of the air conditioner—filling the space around us. It's a comfortable silence.

The class concludes with a relaxation session. As we roll up our mats, I realize how relaxed I feel, not just in body, but in spirit too. There's an ease to my interaction with Max that wasn't there before.

Max stands up, stretching his arms above his head. "You know, I didn't think I'd say this, but I actually enjoyed that. Might not be ready for whatever the yoga version of the NHL is, but it was... good."

His admission makes me smile. "I'm glad you liked it. Maybe we can make this a regular thing."

He raises an eyebrow playfully. "I wouldn't go that far, but I wouldn't say no to another class."

As we walk out of the studio, I find myself replaying the moments from the class in my head—the laughter, the closeness, the shared connection. It's moments like these that blur the lines of our fake engagement, making it feel real, if only for a while.

As we step out into the fresh air, the lightness of the yoga class still lingers between us. Max stretches his arms overhead, a grin on his face.

"That was something," he chuckles. "I haven't felt this relaxed in... well, I can't even remember when."

I laugh along, feeling the remnants of our shared joy. "You did great, despite a few... artistic interpretations of the poses."

Max shoots me a mock-offended look. "Hey, I'll have you know my 'Downward Dog' was a thing of beauty."

"Absolutely," I agree, nodding with exaggerated solemnity. "A masterpiece."

As we stroll down the street, Max glances over at me. "How about we grab something healthy to eat? Keep the whole Zen vibe going?"

"Sounds perfect," I reply, surprised at his suggestion but pleased by it. We decide on a nearby vegan café known for its delicious smoothie bowls and salads.

Walking side by side, I can't help but reflect on the day. There's an ease to our interactions now, a rhythm that feels almost natural. Yet, underlying it all is this complex web of emotions. Happiness at the fun we had, sure, but also confusion. Confusion about what I feel for Max, and apprehension about where this all leads.

The line between our fake relationship and whatever is brewing beneath the surface seems blurrier than ever. The laughter, the glances, the light touches—were they all just for show? Or was there something more genuine in those moments?

As we reach the café and order our food, these thoughts swirl in my mind. Sitting across from Max, watching him talk about his favorite smoothie flavors, I realize that I'm seeing him in a new light. Not just as Max Decker, the hockey star and my fake fiancé, but as someone who's complex, vulnerable, and... real.

But with this newfound connection comes a fresh wave of uncertainty. Our future, both as a couple and as individuals, is as unpredictable as ever. What happens when the fake engagement ends? When the spotlight fades?

24

Max

"YOU'VE NEVER SKATED?" I ask, totally incredulous. The revelation hits me like a stray puck. "How is that possible? It's like a rite of passage here in Cedarwood."

The two of us are at Benny's, a burger-and-shake diner in town. The place is abuzz with the dun of the lunch rush, the scent of fresh fries and searing meat in the air.

Hailey shrugs, a playful smirk on her lips. "Guess I was too busy burying my nose in books to notice the ice."

I lean back, the idea already taking root. "Well, that settles it. We're going ice skating. It's non-negotiable."

Her laughter fills the air, warm and infectious. "Max Decker, the ice-skating evangelist. Alright, I'm in, but I'm warning you, I might be a hazard on the ice."

As we leave the diner, a flood of memories washes over me. I remember our first night together, years ago. The way Hailey looked under the moonlight, the way she laughed, the way she felt in my arms. It was more than just teenage passion; it was the first time I felt something real. But back then, I was too scared to admit it, even to myself.

We arrive at the indoor rink, and I can't help but feel a surge of excitement. This place is more than just ice and boards; it's where I found my purpose, where I escaped the chaos of foster homes.

"This is it," I announce, gesturing grandly to the rink. "The hallowed ground of Cedarwood hockey."

Hailey looks around, her eyes wide with a mix of awe and apprehension. "It's... bigger than I imagined."

I can't help but chuckle. "Wait till you get on the ice. It feels like a whole other world."

I lace up my skates with practiced ease, watching as Hailey struggles with hers. "Here, let me help you with that," I offer, kneeling to tighten her laces.

"Thanks," she says, a hint of nervousness in her voice. "I'm seriously out of my element here."

"Trust me, you'll do great," I reassure her, offering my hand as we step onto the ice.

Hailey's first steps are tentative, her arms flailing for balance. "Oh wow, this is... slippery," she exclaims, teetering dangerously.

I catch her before she can fall, our bodies pressed close. "The trick is to relax and glide," I advise, trying to hide my grin.

"Easy for you to say, Mr. NHL," she retorts, but there's laughter in her voice.

I guide her slowly around the rink, her grip on my arm gradually loosening as she finds her rhythm. "Look at you, Hailey Rogers, natural-born skater," I tease.

She laughs, a sound that fills me with an unexpected warmth. "Don't get ahead of yourself, Decker. I'm still one wrong move from a spectacular wipeout."

The rink becomes our world for the next hour, a small universe of ice and laughter. Hailey clings to me, her grip firm on my arm, her skates carving tentative lines across the smooth surface. Every so often, her footing slips, and she lurches against me, a mix of panic and giggles escaping her.

"You're trying to take me down with you, aren't you?" I tease, steadying her with a gentle pull.

"In your dreams, Decker," she shoots back, her eyes sparkling with mirth. "I wouldn't dream of damaging Cedarwood's precious hockey star."

I can't help but laugh, the sound echoing around the rink. Teaching Hailey to skate is like discovering a hidden chapter of a well-loved book. She's cautious yet adventurous, her laughter a melody that lingers in the cold air.

"Left foot, glide, then right," I instruct, guiding her movements. "You're getting it. Look at you go!"

Her face beams with pride, a flush of excitement coloring her cheeks. "Thanks to my excellent teacher," she says, her tone warm.

As we circle the rink, I find myself opening up more than I intended. I tell her about the countless afternoons and evenings I spent here, how the rink was a haven for me.

"This place was more than just ice. It was where I could be myself, where I felt like I belonged."

Hailey's gaze softens, her eyes lingering on mine. "I had no idea," she whispers, her voice tinged with empathy.

"Yeah, well, not many people do," I admit, feeling an unfamiliar tightness in my chest. "But it made me who I am."

She nods, her hand squeezing mine in a silent gesture of understanding. In that moment, the line between our fake engagement and the real emotions stirring within us blurs further. The playful banter gives way to a more profound connection, a shared understanding of each other's struggles and strengths.

We continue to skate, the sound of our laughter a testament to the unexpected journey we're on together. It's a journey marked by playful teasing and heartfelt confessions, a dance on ice that mirrors the complexity of our relationship.

Hailey's confidence grows by the minute. She's no longer clinging to me for dear life but moving with a grace that surprises us both. Her laughter rings clear and true, a sound that resonates deep within me, stirring emotions I've long kept dormant.

As we glide to a stop at the edge of the rink, our breaths creating small clouds in the cold air, I realize how close we've drifted. Our faces are inches apart, her eyes searching mine, full of questions and something else—something deeper.

For a heartbeat, the world falls away. It's just Hailey and me, and the unspoken tension that's been building between us. My heart pounds in my chest, urging me to close the gap, to taste the lips that have been haunting my dreams since that night years ago.

But before I can act on the impulse, the moment shatters. A chorus of excited voices cuts through the air, and a group of kids skates up to us, their eyes wide with excitement. "Yo, Max Decker! Can we get a picture?"

I can't help but smile, despite the sudden interruption. "Sure, dudes," I say, pulling away from Hailey. The kids swarm around me, their energy and enthusiasm pulling me back to reality.

I steal a glance at Hailey, her cheeks flushed, a small smile playing on her lips. There's a hint of disappointment in her eyes, a mirror of my own feelings. We laugh it off, but the 'what if' hangs between us, an unsaid question that adds another layer to our already complicated relationship.

We skate off the rink, the cool night air hitting us as we step outside. The atmosphere is thick with unspoken words and lingering glances. I want to talk about that almost-kiss, to explore what it means for us, but I hold back. There's already so much at stake, and I can't risk making things more difficult for Hailey, for us.

Hailey seems to be in a similar state of conflict. She's quiet as we walk, her gaze distant, lost in thought. The connection we shared on the ice is undeniable, but so is the complexity of our fake engagement.

We reach the decision to part ways for the evening, each needing time to process the day's events. "I'll see you tomorrow," Hailey says, her voice soft.

"Yeah, see you," I reply, watching her walk away. There's a tightness in my chest, a mix of desire and confusion. Part of me wants to chase after her, to keep this feeling alive, but the rational side holds me back.

As Hailey disappears into the night, I'm left standing there, my mind racing with possibilities and what-ifs. The connection between us is growing stronger, more real, but so are the complications. I can't help but wonder where this path will lead us, whether the fake facade we've built could ever turn into something genuine.

I shove my hands in my pockets, turning away from the rink, the place where I've always felt most at home. But tonight, as I walk back to my hotel room, I realize that home isn't just a place. It's a feeling, a connection. And right now, that feeling is tied up in a woman who's turning my world upside down, in the best and most terrifying way possible.

25

Hailey

THREE WEEKS HAVE WHIZZED by since that morning. In what feels like the blink of an eye, we've transformed our separate lives into a seemingly inseparable existence. People often say that relationships are hard work, but faking one? That's an art form.

We've shared countless candid photos on social media—sunset walks on the beach, cozy dinner dates at the hippest places in town, all sorts of cutesy stuff. It's been important to show the world our united front, to sell the narrative of our whirlwind romance. I've even met his teammates at a charity event where Max was the guest of honor. Being introduced as 'Max Deckers's fiancée' never stops being surreal.

Behind all the glamorous Instagram shots and public outings, the reality is a bit different. We've agreed on certain boundaries to keep our personal and 'professional' lives separate. After all, the whole engagement may be fake, but our individual feelings and vulnerabilities are very much real. We've respected each other's personal space and haven't encroached on those boundaries. Behind closed doors, we've been almost business-like—discussing our next public appearance, coordinating schedules, and ensuring we're always on the same page.

It's a bizarre sort of dance—being intimate in the public eye but distant in private. Yet, as days morph into weeks, there's no denying the familiarity that's creeping in, the ease with which we anticipate each other's moves. However, I keep reminding myself that this is just an act, a ruse. We're just two people playing our parts to perfection. Nothing more... as much as part of me might ache for something more.

The morning sun casts long shadows on the pavement as Max and I make our way down the high street of Cedarwood, the shop windows glistening with the early light. We're on a mission to find the perfect engagement ring. Which is, quite honestly, a sentence I never thought I'd say, especially considering our current situation.

I'm still pretty peeved about Max's casual dismissal of our night together, weeks ago though it may have been. Sure, it was unexpected and maybe ill-advised, but his glib comments just prove that he's still the same old Max. He's arrogant, cocky, and sometimes downright infuriating. But that's neither here nor there right now. We have a ring to buy.

Walking into the first jewelry store, I'm taken aback by the sheer variety of rings available. From solitaires to halos, every cut and design imaginable lies before me. I never considered myself the flashy type. You know, the kind of girl who dreams of a ring that's so big it could double as a weapon. But some of these are admittedly quite captivating.

As I browse through the collection, one ring in particular catches my eye. It's an antique piece, elegantly understated with intricate detailing that reflects its history. The diamond isn't ostentatious, but it's pretty and tasteful.

"That one's really nice," I comment, pointing it out to Max.

He glances over, barely giving it a second before dismissing it. "Nah, it's too simple. We need something big and eye-catching, something that'll make a statement."

I bristle at his tone, the insinuation clear that he knows best. But before I can voice my opinion, he's moved on, captivated by a ring that's the polar opposite of what I had in mind. It's a large, gaudy piece, the diamond so big it's almost comical.

Without so much as asking my opinion, he addresses the sales associate. "We'll take this one."

I blink in surprise. "Wait, what? Max, I don't think—"

"It's perfect," he interrupts, not giving me room to argue. "Trust me."

I press my lips into a thin line, biting back a retort. Fine, if he wants to play it that way, I'll let him. But internally, I'm anything but pleased. The audacity of the man to just make decisions without consulting me. But then again, I remind myself, this engagement isn't real. And yet, despite that logic, a part of me wishes he'd at least pretend to care about my opinion.

We exit the shop, Max looking particularly smug with his purchase. "You'll see, Hailey," he says confidently. "This is going to make a huge splash. Everyone's going to be talking about it."

I roll my eyes. "If by 'talking' you mean making fun of us for such a tacky choice, then sure."

He chuckles, seemingly unfazed by my sarcasm. "Trust me, it's going to be epic."

As we continue down the street, my thoughts wander back to the antique ring. It was beautiful in its own right, a testament to a time gone by. A time where things were simpler and perhaps, more genuine. But as I shake my head, chasing away the sentiment, I reiterate my earlier mantra: The engagement isn't real. No point getting worked up over a piece of jewelry.

But the small voice in the back of my mind nags at me, wondering if Max will ever truly consider my feelings in all of this. As the day wears on, that remains to be seen.

We keep walking in silence. I'm still a bit miffed about the ring, but I remind myself that I need to keep my eyes on the prize—saving the family home. "So, Max," I ask, trying to keep my tone neutral, "What's the next event in this pageant of ours?"

Max checks his phone, his face illuminated by the screen. "Lawrence wants to meet you. My lawyer? We have a lunch reservation at The Elysian."

My eyebrows shoot up in surprise. "The Elysian? Really?" I recall how that place was always out of our family's budget. It's where the well-heeled kids from school would hold their graduation dinners, their sweet sixteen parties. Basically, any occasion where they could flaunt their family's wealth. Going there was something I could never fathom, even in my wildest dreams.

"Yeah, he thought it would be the best place in town. Plus, it's sort of neutral ground for both of us." He winks at me, but I'm too taken aback by our destination to fully appreciate his attempt at humor.

***

Arriving at The Elysian, I feel like I've stepped into another world. The opulence is evident from the plush carpets to the glittering chandeliers. The maitre'd leads us to our table, where a tall, impeccably dressed man waits, nursing a glass of what appears to be very expensive whiskey.

"Lawrence," Max greets, clasping the older man's hand in a firm shake.

"Max," Lawrence replies, his voice smooth but with a hint of haughtiness. His gaze shifts to me, evaluating, almost dissecting. I straighten my back, unwilling to be intimidated. "And you must be Hailey."

I extend my hand, forcing a smile. "That's me. It's nice to meet you."

His handshake is brief, almost dismissive. "Likewise," he says, but his tone suggests otherwise.

As we sit, I can't help but feel the weight of Lawrence's scrutiny. He seems like the type who's been in the business forever, old-school to the core. He's snooty, almost patronizing, and it's evident he's not particularly pleased with Max's choice of fiancée. Well, pretend fiancée, but I doubt that would matter to him.

"This is a quaint little town," Lawrence muses, glancing around the restaurant. "I usually prefer my usual haunts in Chicago, but I suppose this is the best Cedarwood has to offer. Though, I must admit, it's quite beneath my usual standards."

Max clears his throat, shooting Lawrence a warning look. "Cedarwood has its charm."

I bite my lip to hold back a retort. Who is this guy to pass judgment on my hometown? Sure, Cedarwood might not have the glitz and glamour of the big city, but it has heart, and that's something you can't put a price on.

"Anyway," Lawrence says, blowing past the comments. "Let's get to the matter at hand."

We discuss the PR strategy for the 'engagement' and Lawrence has ideas, so many ideas. Each one seems more extravagant than the last. Throughout the meeting, Lawrence's subtle digs continue, aimed not just at Cedarwood but at me as well.

While digging into my salad, I notice Lawrence giving me a particularly pointed look across the table. He sets down his silverware with a precision that screams control and leans in, catching my full attention.

"You know, Hailey," he starts, voice dripping with condescension, "when Max first told me about this... arrangement," he almost spits out the word, "I was skeptical. Not about the engagement itself, but about how seamlessly you seem to have integrated into our world."

I blink, taken aback by the sudden shift in conversation. "I'm sorry, I don't quite—"

He continues, cutting me off, "It's just that, typically, it's my role to handle all of Max's PR, all of his decisions. Yet here you are, making choices, influencing him. It feels as though my job is being... usurped, shall we say."

I can feel the heat rising to my cheeks, indignation bubbling up. Who is he to challenge me this way? I open my mouth to respond, but Lawrence, ever the master of redirection, changes the topic before I can get a word out.

"And the weather, nightmarish isn't it?"

I'm left stunned, my retort trapped in my throat. This man is infuriatingly slick. I take a deep breath, silently reminding myself to pick my battles. Lawrence may have landed a hit, but the game is far from over.

By the time dessert arrives, I'm ready to get out of there. I'm mentally exhausted, having to play nice while being silently judged by Mr. High and Mighty.

When the meeting finally concludes, Max and I step out into the fresh air. The tension from the restaurant seems to dissipate almost instantly, replaced by the comforting familiarity of Cedarwood.

"So," I say, turning to Max with a raised eyebrow. "That was... something."

Max rubs the back of his neck, looking sheepish. "Yeah, sorry about that. Lawrence can be... a lot."

I snort. "That's one way to put it."

Strolling through the familiar streets of Cedarwood with Max, I'm struck by how different the scene feels. Sure, the brick-laid paths and century-old buildings haven't changed, but the gazes upon us certainly have. It's clear that the town's gossip mills are working overtime. Whispers and giggles fill the air as we pass by groups of people, and I can't help but feel a mix of amusement and embarrassment.

Max nudges me playfully, nodding towards a cluster of ladies who are none-too-subtly watching us from a café's patio. "Looks like the secret's out," he grins, obviously enjoying the attention.

"Yeah." I let out a weak laugh and put on an even weaker smile. "Seems like it."

"We'll give them a show to remember tonight," he declares with confidence. The thought of a very public proposal, even a fake one, sends a shiver of apprehension down my spine.

I must've shown my apprehension because Max, ever the opportunist, quickly points to a boutique across the street. "Hey, pick out something nice for tonight, anything you want. It's on me."

The gesture is sweet, but also a little overwhelming. "Are you sure?" I ask, taken aback by his offer. Cedarwood might be small, but its boutiques can be surprisingly pricey.

"Absolutely," he assures, offering a wink. "No expense spared for my soon-to-be fake fiancée."

Before we part ways, I notice Max pausing, a look of hesitation on his face that I haven't seen before. It's as if he's wrestling with something inside, a thought he wants to share but can't quite articulate.

"Max?" I prod gently, curious about his sudden shift in demeanor.

He seems to shake himself from whatever internal debate he was having. "Just... meet me here at six," he says, evading my question and pointing to a spot near the town fountain. "I've got everything planned."

I nod, my curiosity piqued but deciding to let it go.

As I watch him walk away, I can't shake this odd feeling in my chest, a tug of emotions that I hadn't anticipated when we started this crazy charade.

26

Max

The amber liquid from the old-fashioned glass swirls between my lips as I pull up Twitter on my phone, waving it in Lawrence's direction. We're sitting in the dimly lit hotel bar, which offers an ambiance of sophistication I find mildly amusing considering we're in Cedarwood.

"Look at this, Lawrence," I exclaim, barely hiding the glee in my voice. "The engagement bash is trending. Can you believe that? Trending!"

Lawrence takes a sip of his gin and tonic. "Oh?" he asks, his tone dripping with practiced indifference.

My grin widens. "Yeah. And check out the reach these posts are getting. Hailey's been on fire with the whole social media thing. Honestly, I never expected her to be this good at it. Look!"

I shove my phone closer, showing him a recent post Hailey crafted. It's an old high school picture of us. The caption reads: From high school pals to maybe soon-to-be-wed. Who would've guessed?

He scans the post, but I don't miss the clenching of his jaw. "It's charming," he concedes, but there's a certain iciness to the word.

"And that's not all," I continue, excitement building. "Almost everyone from high school is going to be there. I mean, the response has been wild. Who knew our little love story would resonate with so many people?"

Lawrence clears his throat. "It's certainly garnered more attention than I anticipated." His fingers drum on the countertop, the rhythm irregular.

The bartender places a bowl of mixed nuts between us, and I grab a handful. "Oh, come on, Lawrence. Lighten up! This is great press, right? All publicity is good publicity."

He sips his drink again. "While that's generally true, one must also be careful about the narrative being spun. It has to remain in control."

I laugh, a hearty sound echoing in the bar. "Don't worry so much. Hailey's got this. I mean, did you see her latest post on Instagram? The comments are insane!"

But instead of sharing my enthusiasm, Lawrence seems to darken, his usually composed face etched with annoyance. "Max, my job is to worry. To ensure the narrative benefits you, and by extension, me. I appreciate Ms. Rogers's... enthusiasm. But we can't let this spiral out of control."

I shake my head, taking another swig of my drink. "Spiral out of control? Man, you make it sound like we're planning a coup, not an engagement."

He fixes me with a pointed look. "All I'm saying is we need to maintain a certain image, a certain... decorum."

I chuckle. "Always the professional, huh? Don't worry. Tonight's bash will be epic. Just you wait and see."

Lawrence merely nods, but there's a hint of something else in his eyes. Something I can't quite place. But I decide to brush it off. After all, tonight is about celebration and fun.

I lean back in my seat, observing Lawrence closely. There's an unease emanating from him that's impossible to ignore.

"Come on, spill it," I say with a slight smirk, swirling my drink in my hand. "You've got that pinched look on your face like you've sucked on a particularly sour lemon. What gives?"

Lawrence sighs deeply, setting his glass down with a bit more force than necessary. "Max," he starts, clearly picking his words with care. "I have to express my concern about this... this detour you're taking with the PR strategy."

I chuckle, the amusement clear in my voice. "Detour? Lawrence, man, you make it sound like I've veered off into a ditch somewhere."

He shoots me a sharp glance. "In a manner of speaking, perhaps you have. Social media is a tool, not a strategy. And while Ms. Rogers has indeed garnered quite a bit of attention in a short span of time, it's fickle, ephemeral."

I raise an eyebrow. "Fickle? Ephemeral? Lawrence, we've gotten more traction in the past week than we have in the last six months with your... traditional methods."

He scowls, obviously not thrilled with my retort. "Look, I'm just not used to being sidelined, especially when it's in favor of flash-in-the-pan social media trends."

I lean forward, my tone softening. "I get it. But Lawrence, Hailey's methods are working. And it's not just about the trends. It's about engagement, connection. She's tapped into something real here."

He rubs his temples. "Fine. We can debate strategies and methods all night. But there's something else on my mind."

I gesture for him to continue. "Shoot."

Lawrence's demeanor shifts, taking on a more serious tone. "It's about the... arrangement you two have. It should be in writing."

I blink, taken aback. "You want a written agreement for a fake engagement?"

He nods, looking slightly uncomfortable. "Precisely. As your legal counsel, I must insist on it. It's a safeguard."

"Against what?" I ask incredulously.

Lawrence hesitates, searching for the right words. "Look, Max, Hailey's a lovely girl. But... what if things go south? What if she decides to take advantage of the situation? The press, the attention, the wealth..."

I can feel the heat rising in my cheeks. "Lawrence, are you suggesting Hailey would... what? Gold dig?"

Lawrence shifts in his seat, looking slightly embarrassed. "I'm not suggesting anything. But it's my duty to protect your interests. You can't just wear your heart on your sleeve when so much is at stake."

I stare at him, trying to process the enormity of what he's insinuating. "You seriously think she'd do that?"

He meets my gaze steadily. "I've seen it happen, Max. Good people can be tempted by the allure of fame and fortune. I'd hate to see you get hurt."

I let out a frustrated breath, running a hand through my hair. "Fine, draw up whatever you think we need. But just know that I trust Hailey."

Lawrence nods, clearly relieved. "I'll take care of it. It's just a precaution, Max."

I lean back in my chair, suddenly feeling the weight of the very strange situation I'd found myself in.

27

Hailey

"YOU LOOK HOT," LUCY says, brushing her fingers through her wavy hair and giving me a sly wink through the reflection.

I yank at the hem of the dress, my reflection in Lucy's full-length mirror feeling like a stranger. The teal dress, a tight-fitting, off-the-shoulder number, is absolutely not something I'd normally wear. It clings to every curve, and I can't help but feel a little exposed.

"This?" I gesture to my outfit with a frown. "It feels like I'm trying too hard. And it doesn't feel me."

She saunters over, placing a hand on my waist and tilting her head. "Hales, the only thing hard about this situation is how you're not showing off that banging body of yours more often."

I chuckle, shaking my head. "Lucy, I'm not the flaunt-my-assets type."

"Honey," she says with an exaggerated sigh, "there's a difference between flaunting and hiding. And all those baggy tees and jeans and girlboss pantsuits? Definitely hiding."

Staring at my reflection, it feels like I'm peering into some alternate reality. This isn't the Hailey from high school, the one who was more content in her sneakers and oversized sweaters.

Lucy notices my distant gaze. "You okay?"

"I just..." I trail off, lost in thought. "Do you remember how Max used to look at girls back in high school?"

Lucy smirks, "You mean that hungry, I'm-the-king-of-the-world gaze?"

I nod. "I saw that look again, but this time it was directed at me." I bite my lip, feeling heat rise in my cheeks. "It was... intense. It was like there was this undeniable hunger in his eyes, but also... something softer. Almost as if I was the most beautiful woman he'd ever seen."

Lucy raises an eyebrow. "And how did that make you feel?"

Vulnerable. Beautiful. Desired. "Confused," is what I say out loud.

She gives me a knowing look, about to speak when the sharp sound of my phone's timer rings out, breaking the moment.

"Looks like it's time," Lucy says, offering me her arm.

I give my reflection one last glance, taking a deep breath. Maybe it's the tight dress or the soft curls cascading down my back, or perhaps it's the newfound confidence Max's gaze has instilled in me. But I feel better—good even, about the night ahead.

After all, tonight's the night of the big proposal.

"Lucy, I feel ridiculous." I say, adjusting the neckline of my dress and giving her a helpless look. "I mean, this is all just pretend, right? Why am I so anxious?"

She smirks, grabbing a compact mirror from her vanity and touching up her lipstick. "It might be pretend, but let me tell you, being the center of attention is a big deal, especially for someone who would rather blend into the wallpaper at most parties."

I grimace. She's right, of course. I've never been one to step into the spotlight willingly. "It's just... this is a lot."

Lucy stands, walking over to me and placing her hands on my shoulders. "Hales, look at me." I meet her gaze. "You've got this. This evening? It's all about you and Max. And yes, it's fake, but it's also a big, exciting chapter in the story of your life. It's not every day you get to be the lead in your own romantic comedy. Own it!"

Feeling a surge of confidence, I give her a nod. "Alright, I'm owning it." I emphasize the last word with a finger-point for good measure.

"That's the spirit!" Lucy says, clapping her hands together. "Now, get out there and dazzle!"

Feeling bolstered by her pep talk, I hurry down the steps and out the door. The cool evening air greets me as I step onto the sidewalk, but it's Max, leaning against a sleek, black sports car that really takes my breath away.

He's in a tailored charcoal suit that fits him perfectly, with a crisp white shirt and a matte black tie. His shoes, polished to perfection, reflect the evening lights. His dark hair is styled in a casual yet sophisticated manner, making him look more like a GQ model than my old high school acquaintance.

Damn. If I thought I felt something looking in the mirror, seeing Max makes my insides positively quiver. That man cleans up well. Very well.

"Wow," is all I manage to say as I approach.

Max pushes off the car, the corner of his mouth quirking up in a smirk. "You're looking pretty good yourself," he drawls, stepping closer and giving me a once over.

"Thanks," I reply, trying to maintain some semblance of composure.

Without a word, he closes the gap between us and captures my lips with his. It's a soft, yet confident kiss. Brief, but it sends a shiver down my spine.

"We're going to rock this party," he whispers against my lips.

"That kiss wasn't exactly necessary, Max," I quip as he graciously opens the car door for me. "I mean, unless the trees are writing articles about us now." I gesture towards the quiet, empty street.

He blinks, looking momentarily taken aback, but then breaks into a grin. "I'm just... method acting. You know, really getting into the role of doting fiancé. Got to be prepared for when the paparazzi jump out of the bushes."

"Uh-huh. You keep telling yourself that," I laugh, sliding into the plush leather seat.

The inside of the car is just as luxurious as the exterior. I can't help but run my fingers over the soft leather of the seats, impressed despite myself.

Max revs the engine, a soft purr that promises power, and we're off. "So, just wait until you see this party, Hailey. It's going to be epic. Our old classmates won't know what hit them."

I raise an eyebrow. "Epic? Seriously? I was kind of hoping for, you know, a cozy little get-together. Close friends, intimate setting, that sort of thing."

He chuckles, giving me a sidelong glance. "You kidding? A night like tonight? No way we're doing low-key. I want the world talking about it. Trust me, this is going to be a night to remember."

"I just thought, maybe, for once, something could be real between us," I reply, more to myself than to him.

Max's jovial demeanor falters for a split second. "It's all about appearances," he says, more business-like now. "Gotta give the people what they want, and they want spectacle."

My gut tightens. Appearances. Right. That's what this is all about.

"Besides," he continues with a roguish grin, trying to lighten the mood, "you'll be the belle of the ball. Everyone's eyes will be on you."

I sigh, looking out of the window. "Since when have I ever been the kind of woman to want that?"

The tension between us is palpable as we pull up to the Cedarwood Grand. The party's all the way at the very top, and I can see the strings of fairy lights from all the way down at street level, the din of conversation and music wafting down to greet us. My heart sinks as I see the sheer number of cars outside. Max wasn't kidding—this is no intimate gathering.

The valet opens my door, and I step out, suddenly feeling very exposed in my tight dress. I can hear the low hum of voices, laughter, and music emanating from the venue. It's clear this isn't just a reunion of high school friends, but a full-blown media event.

I turn to Max, searching his eyes for some reassurance, some sign that he understands how overwhelmed I feel. But he's all business, his face a mask of practiced charm.

"Ready?" he asks, offering me his arm.

I swallow hard, pushing down the rising panic. "As I'll ever be," I reply, taking a deep breath.

I'm following Max's lead, trying to hold my head high, but this isn't how I'd ever imagined the night someone would propose to me would be like. I mean, I'm not naïve. I never expected to be riding on a white horse with some prince by my side, but maybe... just a little more intimate than this?

Every step feels like a trek as the weight of dozens of eyes press down on me, judging, evaluating. The noise of chatter and laughter forms a constant hum, punctuated occasionally by a recognizable voice calling out a greeting. Max, of course, laps it all up, waving, shaking hands, and sharing boisterous laughs with anyone and everyone.

But I'm a little out of my depth. The intense spotlight, the shimmering gowns, and tailored suits, the subtle—and not so subtle—nods to our alleged relationship. The fact that Max seems to keep disregarding my feelings, overriding my preferences with a casual shrug and smile, does little to help.

It irks me, and I keep telling myself: it's not real. This isn't a real engagement. But oddly, that thought isn't as comforting as I'd hoped it'd be.

Maybe because some part of me wants it to be real? I shake off the thought as ridiculous.

As I step into the engagement party, the chatter and music swirl around me, a lively sea of faces. But it's the familiar ones that immediately catch my eye. Over by the window, I spot Jake and my parents, looking sharp and polished. My dad's in a crisp suit that I don't remember ever seeing him wear before, and my mom's sky blue dress sparkles subtly in the party lights.

Just beyond my family, I spot Lucy, impossible to miss in a vibrant, eye-catching, mauve party dress that clings in all the right places. As always, she's the picture of vivacity, her laughter floating over the din as she chats animatedly with a group of guests. Her infectious energy is a beacon, just the sight of her doing wonders to quell the anxiety pooling in my belly.

Jake, usually so casual, is dressed in a navy tailored jacket that makes him look more mature. They're engaged in animated conversation with some guests, and just seeing them there, amid all the unfamiliarity, eases the weight in my chest. It's a much-needed relief amidst the whirlwind of the night.

Max, with his wide, ever-present grin, already seems to be having the time of his life. But why wouldn't he? He's always been the center of attention, effortlessly charming and all too aware of it. The kind of guy who doesn't mind being the eye of the storm, often creating it himself.

However, for a girl like me, who prefers quiet nights in with a good book or deep, intimate conversations with close friends, this is borderline nightmarish. I've never been the belle of the ball, and quite frankly, I've never wanted to be.

A photographer pushes through the crowd, camera flash lighting up the space as he snaps away. I try to give my most natural smile, but I can feel it's strained.

"Come on, Hailey! Lighten up!" Max whispers into my ear, his hand finding the small of my back. The touch, however brief, sends a wave of warmth up my spine. I take a deep breath.

"Sorry," I say, "This just isn't... my style."

He cocks an eyebrow, his dazzling smile dimming for a split second, a rare moment of vulnerability peeking through. "Well, for what it's worth, you look stunning, and you're handling this way better than I thought."

I chuckle, "Oh, so you expected me to run screaming into the night?"

His grin returns, full force. "I wouldn't have blamed you if you did."

It's a skill, trying to find a corner to hide in when you're the alleged belle of the ball. A dark corner, perhaps, with a strategic potted plant for extra coverage? But before I can put my brilliant escape plan into action, there's a sudden change in the ambiance. The chatters dim and Max is gone. I turn to see him standing confidently in the center of the room, that familiar mischievous twinkle in his eye.

"Oh no, he's not going to... He wouldn't," I say to myself, the anxiety gnawing at the pit of my stomach. But he clearly has different ideas.

Ladies and gentlemen," he begins in that charming voice of his, amplified by the hush that has descended on the room, "thank you all for coming tonight. As you know, this is not just any party. Tonight is a special night."

Oh, please. Not now, not yet. I'm internally praying he would segue into a toast or a bad joke. But who am I kidding? This is Max. Mr. Showstopper.

"I'm a man of action, and I hate keeping things waiting," he continues, his voice filled with mischief, yet somehow sincere. "I know most of you were expecting a grand build-up, a climax towards the end of the night." He glances in my direction, the corners of his lips turning upwards slightly, as if we share a secret joke. "But why wait?"

The collective gasps are audible, and it feels like my heart is now performing a flamenco in my chest.

"In front of all of you, friends, family, and... fellow Cedarwoodians," he quips, drawing a chuckle from the crowd, "I want to ask a very special question."

Before I know it, he's there, right in front of me, closing the distance between us in a few smooth strides. There's a whirlwind of emotions in his eyes—mischief, yes, but also warmth, vulnerability, and dare I think, love?

Oh shit.

Down on one knee, like some hero from a cheesy rom-com, he holds out that gaudy ring, the one I hadn't particularly cared for. The fairy lights sparkle off the oversized gem, making it look even more ostentatious. It's almost comical.

"Hailey Rogers," he says, voice suddenly soft, intimate, just for me, "Will you do me the honor of becoming my wife?"

Every single eye in the room is on me. I can almost hear the collective holding of breath, the weight of expectation pressing down. My mouth is suddenly dry, words lodged somewhere deep in my throat. Here I am, center stage in a drama I never auditioned for.

In a whirl of emotions, thoughts race: it's not real, it's just for show, you knew this was coming. Yet, nothing could've prepared me for this moment. My brain's screaming one thing, my heart another, and all I can do is stand there, frozen.

28

Max

TIME FREEZES AS I balance on one knee, holding the ridiculously opulent ring out to Hailey. The entire room's hushed, waiting, and for a split-second, my usual unflappable confidence teeters. She's just... standing there, eyes wide, and I swear if I could hear a pin drop over the roaring in my ears, I would.

Did I miscalculate? Is she going to leave me hanging in front of everyone, having second thoughts about this whole, crazy plan?

The tension in the room is palpable. I can hear someone's drink clinking against their glass, the sound amplified in the oppressive silence.

But then, as though pulled from a trance, Hailey's face softens. A tentative, slightly quizzical smile forms on her lips. "Yes, Max. I will."

There we go.

The crowd erupts into applause, wolf-whistles, and cheers. The relief coursing through me is so strong I almost stumble back. But not today. Today, I'm the leading man.

In one fluid move, I'm up on my feet, sliding the gaudy ring onto her slender finger. The fit's like it was made for her.

"See? Perfect," I whisper for her ears only.

Then, getting carried away in the moment, I lean in and plant a deep, theatrical kiss on her lips. The crowd loves it, but I can feel her go stiff in my arms. She's not returning the kiss, not really. It's more of a polite acceptance than the fiery connection we shared the other night.

Breaking away, I shoot her my most charming grin, but I'm left with a niggling feeling that something's off. Did I push it too far? Maybe the public display wasn't her thing. Or maybe, just maybe, there's more to Hailey's feelings about this whole charade than she's letting on.

But for now, the crowd's here, the spotlight's on, and showtime isn't over.

"Let's hear it for the future Mrs. Decker!" I call out, lifting her hand in the air, champion-style. The applause and cheers rise again, and we're surrounded by friends and well-wishers. The energy's infectious.

Yet, amidst all the celebration, I can't shake off the thought of that tension I felt when our lips met. Hailey's an enigma, and I'm suddenly very keen on figuring her out. But for tonight, the show must go on.

The party's in full swing, and I'm loving every second of it. The room's filled with a mix of old friends and new faces, everyone trying to get a piece of the newly engaged couple.

"Max, you old dog!" Jake comes up, clapping me on the back with a grin that rivals mine. "Who would've thought you'd finally settle down?"

"Only took a decade and your amazing sister," I joke, nodding towards Hailey, who's currently engaged in conversation with a group of Cedarwood high school alumni.

The hours fly, and as the night deepens, I notice a change in Hailey. She's more reserved than when we first walked in. At first, I chalk it up to exhaustion. It's been a whirlwind day, after all. But every time I catch her eye, I sense something's not right.

Unfazed, I walk up to her, intending to pull her into the celebration. "Hey! You okay?"

She offers a thin smile, nodding. "Just taking it all in."

Then, the unmistakable opening of Gotye's 'Somebody That I Used To Know' fills the air. An idea pops into my mind, and I can't help the wide grin that forms on my face.

"Ah! Our song!" I exclaim, pulling her towards the makeshift dance floor.

She stumbles a little, caught off guard. "What do you mean, 'our song'?" Her voice carries a hint of incredulity.

"You know," I chuckle, twirling her around, "because it's all about ex-lovers and, well, we're fake lovers. Get it?"

Hailey doesn't seem to share my amusement. Instead, her face goes an odd shade of red, her eyes glancing away. "Max," she says, voice tight, "I think I need a moment."

Before I can respond, she's extricating herself from my grip, weaving her way through the crowd towards the exit. I stand there, stunned, watching her retreat. The festive mood suddenly feels a whole lot less festive.

Jake sidles up next to me, watching Hailey's disappearing form. "Bro, what did you say?"

I shrug, genuinely puzzled. "Just tried to have some fun with her."

Jake shakes his head, clapping me on the back. "Whatever you said, it doesn't look like she thought it was fun. Want me to talk to her?"

"Nah, I got it. Thanks, future bro-in-law."

He laughs, shaking his head as if in disbelief as he walks away.

I nod, taking a deep breath. As the party continues around me, I can't help but feel like I've missed a beat somewhere. It was just a song, a joke. What could have upset her so much?

But as I watch the spot where Hailey vanished, a sinking feeling begins to form in my gut. Maybe this fake engagement is hitting closer to home for her than I realized. Whatever it is, I intend to find out.

The door to the rooftop makes a soft click as I push through it, revealing a breathtaking vista. Cedarwood lies sprawled below, its vintage homes and streets lit up, creating a beautiful contrast with the darkness. To the east, the towering cedar trees the town is named after stand sentinel, their ancient silhouettes bathed in moonlight. And to the west, the vast expanse of the ocean, its waves glistening, making me wish for a moment of solitude to just take it all in.

But my attention is elsewhere.

Hailey sits alone at the edge, her silhouette outlined against the panoramic backdrop. Even from this distance, I can sense a change in her demeanor—a certain vulnerability that wasn't there before.

I approach cautiously, my footsteps echoing on the concrete floor. "Hey," I start, my tone softer than I intended.

She doesn't answer right away. Instead, she continues to look out over the town, her gaze distant, her thoughts clearly elsewhere.

There's a tension between us, palpable, and for once, my usually quick wit fails me. "Is everything okay?" I finally manage.

She takes a moment, her eyes still fixed on the horizon. "It's... nothing," she says finally, her voice distant.

The silence stretches on, and I find myself shifting uncomfortably. That cocky, confident part of me wants to crack a joke, to lighten the mood, but another part of me knows better. Hailey's always been an enigma to me, but right now, she feels more distant than ever.

Suddenly, she stands, her dress catching the breeze. "We should head back," she says, her tone detached, professional. "We have appearances to keep."

I watch her for a moment, trying to decipher the sudden change. She's always been the more reserved one, but this feels different. Cold, almost.

"Hailey," I begin, trying to find the words. "If there's something bothering you, you can talk to me."

She glances at me, her emerald eyes searching mine for a moment before looking away. "It's nothing, Max. Just... let's get back to the party."

And with that, she turns and heads towards the door, leaving me standing there, more puzzled than ever. As the door clicks shut behind her, I'm left with a sinking feeling that I've just missed something very, very crucial.

29

Hailey

Walking into the Cedarwood Grand's Presidential Suite, the soft glow of our phones immediately illuminates the space, casting shadows that dance around as we move. It's all a bit surreal, honestly. A few weeks ago, I was just a regular girl, and now, I'm some sort of... internet sensation.

Taking a quick peek at my phone, I can see notifications rolling in. Twitter, Instagram, even Facebook. There's no escaping it. Pictures of the party, the proposal—every little detail—are plastered all over the internet. And smack in the center of all this madness? Me. Hailey Rogers, small-town girl turned overnight sensation. I mean, who would've thought?

Max, on the other hand, seems totally in his element, scrolling through his feed with a smug grin plastered across his face. Typical. He approaches me, brandishing his phone like it's a prized possession.

"Here, this is the one I was looking for!" he exclaims, shoving his screen into my face.

I squint at the image, and oh, there I am—eyes wide, jaw slack, the very picture of surprise and, well, utter disbelief. It's not my best look.

"Really? *This* is the picture you were hunting for?" I say, my tone dripping with sarcasm.

He chuckles, that signature cocky grin stretching across his face. "Absolutely! Look at you! So shocked, so... genuine."

Rolling my eyes, I huff. "You know, that was a real dick move, Max. We had a plan! You were supposed to propose later in the night."

He shrugs nonchalantly, leaning against the wall with a smirk. "Look, Hailey, you're brilliant and beautiful and all that, but I had to make sure that reaction was genuine. Didn't think I could rely on those acting skills of yours."

I resist the urge to smack him. "Oh, so ambushing me was your grand plan?"

His eyes dance with mischief. "Worked, didn't it?"

I take a deep breath, trying to remain calm, despite the swirling emotions inside me. "You're impossible," I mutter, half-annoyed and half-amused.

Max winks. "And yet, here we are."

He holds up a finger.

"Wait here. I'll get us something to celebrate with," Max grins, sauntering off to fetch a bottle of bubbly. As the door clicks shut behind him, I find myself enveloped by the silence. It's just me and my thoughts.

Classic Max. Everything has to be about him. The proposal, the jokes, the whole damn engagement—even if it's fake. I understand that we're in this together, but sometimes it feels like I'm just a supporting actress in the Max Show. It's the same disregard he showed me back in high school, the same nonchalance.

And the song? That song was *our* song, the song that'd been playing when I'd given myself to him. Did he even care? Or even worse, did he even remember?

Playing it as a joke, especially considering its significance, felt like a punch to the gut. Maybe for him, that night was just another conquest, but for me, it was monumental. For him to trivialize it like that... Well, it stings.

I'm jarred out of my thoughts as Max returns, brandishing a bottle of champagne, and two glasses. "For us!" he proclaims, popping the bottle open with a flourish.

"To our fake engagement," I quip, trying to hide the bitterness in my voice.

As he pours the champagne into the glass, the bubbles rush to the surface, mimicking the tumult of emotions churning within me. I lift the glass to my lips, ready for a sip, but suddenly, a wave of nausea sweeps over me. I set the glass down, trying to shake off the feeling.

Max notices my discomfort. "What's wrong?" he asks, genuine concern in his eyes.

"It's... nothing," I reply, forcing a smile. "Just not feeling the alcohol tonight."

He raises an eyebrow. "You sure you're alright? You seem a little off."

I resist the urge to snap back. Instead, I try to change the topic. "It's been a long day. I think I'll just get some rest."

Max smirks, wiggling his eyebrows suggestively. "I'd suggest we share the bed again, but considering what happened last time..."

I roll my eyes, not in the mood for his antics. "Max, I'm taking the couch."

He laughs as he pulls off his shirt and kicks off his shoes.

For a moment, we're both silent, the weight of the day's events pressing down on us.

There's so much on my mind, so much weighing me down. No sense in trying to puzzle it out all at once. I pull a blanket over myself, and settle in on the couch, hoping for a night of undisturbed sleep—not to mention a clearer head when I wake up in the morning.

***

Stretching as I attempt to shake off the remnants of sleep, I sit up groggily. The unexpected noise has my heart beating a bit faster, and I pull the blanket closer around me to ward off the morning chill. Rubbing the sleep from my eyes, I glance over at Max, who's beaming like he just won the lottery.

For a split second, my mind wanders, and I can't help but take in his physique. Damn, he looks good. The skin-tight boxer-briefs leave very little to the imagination. His abs, chest, everything is on full display. It's annoying how just seeing him like this sends an unexpected warmth flooding through me.

"Morning to you too," I retort sarcastically, shoving down the feeling. "Would you care to put on some pants before you have a full-blown conversation with me?"

He looks down, seemingly just noticing his state of undress, and smirks. "What? Am I distracting you?"

Before I can reply with a scathing comeback, he continues. "Guess what? Reebok wants to meet! They want to renegotiate my contract."

His enthusiasm is infectious, but I'm still trying to piece together what's happening. "Wow, that was fast."

"Well," he says, pausing for dramatic effect. "They specifically want to meet you too. Looks like our little engagement stunt is paying off big time."

I raise an eyebrow. "Guess the plan's working so far. People are buying the whole fake engagement?"

He winks. "Of course, they are. Why wouldn't they? To the world, I'm now the reformed bad boy, engaged to his hometown sweetheart. A real-life fairytale, and they're buying it."

I groan. "So, you're saying they want to meet with *us*? As in, the happy couple?"

"Exactly." Max grins triumphantly. "And we need to play our parts to perfection."

Before I can voice my concerns, Max, still in his boxer-briefs, saunters over and tosses a pair of pants onto my lap. "Here, get dressed. We've got a big day ahead."

My mind races. The very idea of going into such a high-profile meeting with him, to play a role that I'm still coming to terms with, is daunting. Yet, there's a part of me that's intrigued by the challenge.

"Just a heads up, Max," I start, gathering my bearings, "If we're going into this meeting, I want to be clear on our game plan. I don't want any more surprises."

He nods in agreement, "Understood. We'll strategize before we head out. But first, get dressed."

As he turns to give me some privacy, I can't help but steal one more glance at him. Despite all the chaos and unpredictability that seems to revolve around Max, there's an undeniable magnetic pull between us. I shake my head, trying to clear my thoughts.

"Alright, my oh-so-dashing fiancé," I say, struggling to keep the lightness in my tone, "Let's get this show on the road."

30

Max

I STRAIGHTEN MY TIE as Hailey and I step into the downtown office suite. The plush carpets and gleaming furniture scream big money. But right now, all I can focus on is Hailey. Damn, she looks good in that tailored skirt and blazer combo she changed into. It's making me wonder if these corporate offices have any... private rooms.

I feel a prickly gaze on me and turn to find Lawrence eyeing Hailey with evident curiosity. "Max," he hisses in that 'I'm-totally-being-discreet-but-not-really' tone he always uses, "why is she here?"

"They want to meet her," I respond with a wink. "Guess they want to see in-person the woman who's made an honest man out of me." I nudge him, trying to keep the mood light.

Hailey laughs. "Honest indeed."

Lawrence looks unimpressed, shaking his head as we step out of the elevator.

As we enter the conference room, Hailey gives me a sharp glance. I'm sure she's caught me staring, but hell, can you blame a guy? I've always admired confidence, and she wears it like a second skin. Her chin is high, shoulders back, and that red lip she's rocking? Oh man.

A stern-looking man in glasses stands to greet us, extending a hand. "James Wilde," he begins, his voice carrying the weight of many closed deals and cutthroat negotiations.

"Call me Max," I interject with a smile, giving his hand a firm shake.

"And I'm Lawrence Whitfield, Max's attorney," Lawrence adds quickly, not to be outdone. He extends his own hand.

The stern man's gaze shifts to Hailey, and there's a flicker of... something. Interest? Surprise? Both? "And you are?"

Hailey flashes her brightest, most disarming smile, the one I'm sure has made countless men's hearts skip a beat. "Hailey Rogers. Though, I guess I should start getting used to calling myself Hailey Rogers-Decker." She's the picture of poise and confidence, and as she presses flesh I realize how lucky I am to get a glimpse of her professional side.

"Congratulations, by the way," Wilde says. "To both of you."

A tall woman with a sleek bob and piercing blue eyes comes over next. She nods her acknowledgment. "I'm Carol Vasquez, head of legal with Reebok. Pleasure to meet you all. And congrats."

With introductions out of the way, we all settle into our seats, the large mahogany table making me feel like I'm about to play a high-stakes poker game. I give Hailey one last appreciative glance, hoping she understands that it's not just her killer outfit I'm grateful for.

I lean back in my chair, steepling my fingers as the Reebok suits drone on about brand image and 'influential growth dynamics' or some other corporate mumbo-jumbo. But the one phrase that catches my ear is 'wild bachelor antics.' Ha! If they only knew half of it. Still, it's a nice reminder that those days are behind me.

I sneak a glance at Hailey and can't resist grinning.

"Those days are long gone," I confirm confidently, giving Hailey's hand a reassuring squeeze. Her fingers feel warm and strong in mine, and I feel a heady sense of pride knowing she's with me.

Carol, Ms. Sleek Bob, starts talking numbers, and that definitely gets my attention. "Given your current trajectory and, of course, considering the positive publicity around your recent engagement," she begins, casting a pointed look at Hailey, "we're willing to offer an... enhanced contract."

She slides a glossy print-out across the table, and my eyes nearly pop out of their sockets when I see the figures. It's way more than what I've been making, a figure with a lot of zeros and a substantial signing bonus. There are even clauses about royalties for custom skates and additional incentives based on performance metrics.

Lawrence scans the print-out quickly, nodding his approval. "This looks fine," he says, his tone suggesting he's satisfied.

But Hailey's sharp eyes narrow as she examines another page of the document. I watch as her delicate brow furrows, a clear sign that something's amiss.

"Hang on a sec," she says, her voice low and firm. "What's this clause here about exclusivity rights and third-party endorsements?"

Carol clears her throat, shifting uncomfortably. "Ah, that. It's just a standard clause. It ensures that while you're with Reebok, you won't engage with any other brand for endorsements, even outside the sports realm."

I raise an eyebrow. "That's pretty extensive, don't you think?"

Hailey chimes in, her tone all business. "Especially given this sub-clause which implies a penalty for any kind of breach, even unintentional ones."

Lawrence's face pales a bit as he re-reads the section Hailey's pointed out. "I must've missed that," he admits, looking a tad embarrassed.

Carol sighs, "We can discuss modifications to that clause, but it's generally a part of our standard contracts for top-tier athletes."

Hailey gives her a challenging look, but I'm too engrossed in the sudden twist in the room to intervene. I knew bringing Hailey was a good idea, but man, she just made Lawrence, a Harvard-trained lawyer, look like a rookie.

"Let's table that clause for now," I suggest, flashing a confident smile, "and focus on the rest. But know this," I add, pointing at the questionable section, "we'll be revisiting that with a fine-tooth comb."

In the wake of Hailey's revelation, I can't help but revel in the slightly off-balance demeanor of the Reebok reps. The air in the room is thick with unspoken acknowledgement: they tried to pull a fast one on me, and Hailey was the one to catch them.

"So," I say, leaning back in my chair with a sly grin, "while we're on the subject of additional bonuses and terms, there's something else I've been thinking about."

The Reebok team looks at me expectantly. They probably think it's another demand for more money or privileges.

"I want to funnel a chunk of my signing bonus into a charity package," I declare, watching their faces go from wary to genuinely intrigued.

"That's... unexpected," Carol remarks, looking both surprised and pleased.

"I've been thinking about it for a while. It's about giving back, you know?" I shrug, trying to sound nonchalant even though it means a lot to me. "I was thinking of some local charities, particularly those supporting businesses in Cedarwood."

Hailey's eyes soften, and she gifts me a small, knowing smile. She gets it, realizing that this is the dog-eared money for her family.

Carol nods in agreement, "We can definitely work on that. Reebok is always eager to be involved in initiatives that make a difference."

With the main points of the meeting wrapped up, we all rise, shaking hands and promising to touch base soon. As the Reebok team departs, I turn my attention to Lawrence, who's now looking a tad sheepish, and not at all pleased.

"I can't believe I missed that clause," he grumbles, more to himself than to anyone else.

Hailey raises an eyebrow, "It was pretty glaring, Lawrence. Contracts 101."

The tension between them is palpable. I can practically see the sparks flying. Lawrence's face reddens as he retorts, "I had everything under control. You didn't need to embarrass me like that."

Hailey's about to respond, her stance defensive and her lips parted, when suddenly her face goes pale. Her eyes widen in panic, and she clamps a hand over her mouth.

"Hailey?" I exclaim, concerned.

Without a word, she turns on her heel and sprints to the restroom, leaving Lawrence and me in a stunned silence. Whatever tension there was a moment ago is completely forgotten, replaced by a rising sense of worry. What the hell just happened?

31

Hailey

I'M SITTING IN THE sterile room of Dr. Marion Kelley's office, the familiar pastel paintings of Cedarwood landscapes on the walls. I remember them vividly from when I was a kid, coming in with scraped knees and the occasional flu. Dr. Kelley, with her short curly salt-and-pepper hair and those retro cat-eye glasses she never seemed to part with, was my go-to for all medical woes.

She enters the room, and I stand, feeling suddenly like that eight-year-old girl with chickenpox. "Hailey! It's been ages," she exclaims warmly, hugging me.

"Yeah," I laugh nervously. "A few more inches, a couple more pounds, and a whole lot more life problems, but it's still me."

Dr. Kelley chuckles, "That's the spirit. Now, what brings you here today? Your fiancé mentioned you weren't feeling well when he made the appointment."

God, it was so bizarre hearing Max Decker referred to in that way.

After the little incident with his lawyer, Max had insisted on setting up a doctor's visit for that afternoon. I have to admit, his concern was sweet.

I cringe inwardly, the humiliation from the meeting incident resurfacing. "Just a little spell of nausea, but I'm sure it's nothing."

She nods, scribbling something down. "Well, let's make sure everything's alright. Have there been any other recent changes? Weight gain, changes in appetite, fatigue?"

I shrug, "I mean, I've been tired, but who isn't these days?"

She raises an eyebrow, giving me that doctorly 'I know something you don't' look. "What about your sexual activity?"

I choke on my own spit. "Excuse me?"

She doesn't miss a beat. "Your sex life, Hailey. Have there been any recent... encounters I should be aware of? I know it's a little awkward to discuss, but it's important to know."

My cheeks must be fifty shades of red by now. "Well, I am engaged. But we used protection."

I pause after I speak. Did we?

"Of course, silly me." She nods, scribbling away. "Alright. I'd recommend taking a pregnancy test, just to rule it out."

My heart stops. "A pregnancy test? But... we're not planning on a kid right now, and, and... Oh my God."

Dr. Kelley pats my hand soothingly. "Deep breaths, dear. It's just a precaution."

It's a whole lot more than a precaution, it's my life potentially flipping upside down. But I try to keep it together, giving her a shaky nod.

"Good girl," she says, and there's that familiar comforting tone I remember from childhood. "Let's get this sorted."

And just like that, I'm thrust into the whirlwind of 'What ifs.' What if I am? What will Max say?

Waiting for the results feels like a lifetime. The pastel landscapes on the walls seem to blur into an indistinct mush of colors. I tap my foot anxiously. It can't be, it just can't be. But the universe seems to have other plans for me today. Dr. Kelley walks in with an expression I can't quite read, and my heart starts racing.

"Well," she begins, taking off her glasses and cleaning them with the corner of her white coat, a habit I remember from childhood. "Congratulations, Hailey. You're pregnant."

The room spins. This can't be happening. Not now. I grab the edge of the examination table to keep myself upright. "Are you... sure?"

She nods, giving me a gentle smile. "Quite sure. And I understand it's a shock, but I must say, it's quite the lovely surprise for your fiancé."

I laugh, a manic, awkward sound. "Fiancé," I echo. Right, the world still thinks I'm about to marry Max. A fake engagement, a real pregnancy, and a world watching every move. What could possibly go wrong?

Dr. Kelley gently pats my knee. "There's nothing quite as radiant as a pregnant bride, dear. You'll be glowing on your big day."

I force a smile, even as my mind races. "Thank you, Dr. Kelley. I just... I need some time to process."

"Of course," she says, standing up. "Take all the time you need. We're here for you."

I nod my thanks and hurry out, wanting to escape the clinic and find a quiet corner to just breathe.

As I leave Dr. Kelley's office, my thoughts whirring from the unexpected news, I almost collide with Lawrence. He looks down at me, an inscrutable expression on his sharp face.

"Hailey," he drawls, looking me up and down. "Good to see you. What brings you downtown?" His eyes flick to the front of the doctor's office, then back to me.

I straighten my back, trying to mask my anxiety. "None of your business, Lawrence. What are you doing here?"

He smirks. "Just looking out for my client's best interests." His eyes narrow. "Listen," he starts, leaning in closer so I can feel his stale coffee breath, "I've tolerated your little stunt back with Reebok, but let's not pretend you're anywhere near my level. Stick to whatever it is you do, and leave the real work to the professionals."

A smirk plays on my lips. "Is that a threat, Lawrence? Because I don't appreciate threats."

He takes a step back, his icy blue eyes scanning mine. "Just a friendly piece of advice. You're playing in the big leagues now, Hailey. I suggest you don't overreach."

I laugh. It's a genuine, amused laugh. "Funny, coming from you. From what I've seen, Max could use someone who actually pays attention to detail. If I were you, I'd step up my game."

For a split second, his cool facade falters, but it's quickly replaced by that trademark smug smile of his. "Careful, Hailey," he murmurs, his voice dripping with condescension. "You're playing a dangerous game."

I take a step closer to him, ensuring we're at eye level. "Don't mistake my kindness for weakness, Lawrence. And don't ever threaten me like that again."

He chuckles, but there's no warmth in the sound. "We'll see," he says, letting the words hang in the air like a dark cloud. With that, he saunters off, leaving me with a feeling of unease.

I watch his retreating figure for a moment, my resolve only strengthened. Lawrence may have plans, but so do I.

Whatever game he's got in mind, I'm not backing down.

32

Max

IT'S FUNNY HOW LIFE goes. A week ago, I was Mr. Independence, living my life with more freedom than a bald eagle on a jet ski. Now? I'm fake-engaged, sitting across from a woman whose unreadable expression makes a poker champion look like an open book.

We're dining in a small, candlelit corner one of Cedarwood's most sought-after restaurants—Le Cedar Gourmet. It's intimate, it's classy, and right now, it feels more like an interrogation room.

Hailey's looking... well, damn it, she's looking radiant, but something's off. Her thoughts seem to be elsewhere, and for someone usually so present, it's disconcerting.

"You okay there?" I ask, trying to bring that spark back into her eyes. "You seem like you're a million miles away."

She offers me a thin-lipped smile that doesn't seem genuine. "Just a lot on my mind."

I try to lighten the mood, "You know, in our whirlwind week of paparazzi and Reebok boardroom drama, I've come to realize something.

I miss the old days. Back when our biggest concerns were dodging Mrs. Patterson's scowl or sneaking an extra dessert from the cafeteria."

She chuckles, but it's muted. It feels like I'm performing CPR on our conversation, trying to keep it alive.

Then, there's the elephant in the room. Or, should I say, the wineglass on the table. It's been untouched.

"You not drinking tonight?" I ask, nodding at the still-full glass.

She glances at it, as if seeing it for the first time, then meets my gaze. "Oh, just... not in the mood tonight, I guess."

"Mood?" I arch an eyebrow, fighting the smile playing at the corners of my mouth. "Nervous about something?"

She gives me a side-eye, "You wish. But no, just taking a break for tonight."

My mind races with possibilities. Is she telling me the truth? Or maybe she's worried about something happening between us if she were to get tipsy. We do have a habit of tripping and ending up in bed together these days.

The old Max would've made a cheeky comment, but something's stopping me now. Instead, I reach across the table, taking her hand. It's warm, but her grip is tenuous.

"Hey, whatever it is, we're in this together," I say, trying to reassure her.

She offers a soft smile, squeezing my hand back, and it feels like a tiny win.

But still, there's a nagging feeling at the back of my mind. She's not telling me something,

Well, color me intrigued and slightly panicked.

"Hey, come on," I say, trying to rally her spirits. "Think about it! We get to have all the fun of a wedding without any of the strings attached. We'll have a blast, pull the wool over everyone's eyes, and then? Freedom."

I thought bringing up the fake wedding would be a lighthearted way to deal with our situation. Man, was I wrong.

Her silverware clinks against the plate as she pushes her food around. "Max," she starts, taking a deep breath, "have you ever considered that maybe, just maybe, this isn't as easy for me as it is for you?"

I'm taken aback. "I... I thought we were both in this together. We made a deal. You get to save your parents' business and I keep my image clean. Win-win."

She sighs, placing her napkin neatly beside her plate, her movements deliberate. "It's just..." She pauses, looking for the right words. "You talk about our 'separate ways' like it's no big deal, but maybe..." Her voice trails off and she shakes her head, as if shaking off her thoughts.

I lean in, trying to catch her gaze, "But maybe what?"

She hesitates, biting her lip. "Never mind."

We finish our meal in near silence. The lively atmosphere of the restaurant, the gentle hum of conversations, and the clinking glasses form a stark contrast to our bubble of quiet.

I pull her close as we step out, feeling the cool evening air. The moment seems ripe for one of those Hollywood kisses, one to get people talking, so I lean in, letting my lips brush hers. But the spark? It's not there.

She pulls away, her voice softer than I've ever heard. "I'll see you at the hotel room," she murmurs.

"Wait, aren't we going together?" I ask, a tad bit desperate to keep the evening from ending on such an off note.

"I need to clear my head," she replies, her eyes shadowed, "I'll be okay."

I watch as she hails a cab, leaving me on the curb, feeling like a lead character who's lost the plot. The night's sky is vast and star-studded, but right now, it doesn't hold a candle to the universe of confusion within me.

This was supposed to be simple. No strings, no attachments, just a clear business deal. Yet, here I am, second-guessing every word, every touch. Maybe, just maybe, things between Hailey and me are a lot more tangled than I thought.

There I am, still swimming in the ocean of my thoughts, when the shrill ringtone of my phone slices through the quiet. The screen flashes "Lawrence."

"Lawrence? What's up?" I answer, my tone an odd mix of irritated and curious.

"You know, Max," he begins, every word dripping with condescension, "I was just perusing the revised contract from Reebok, and I noticed that you've handed the whole thing over to Hailey. Your small-town sweetheart."

I can practically see the sneer on his face. "She's good at it, Lawrence. Sharp, and knows both the PR and legal stuff inside out. It's a great combo."

Lawrence scoffs. "I've been handling your contracts for years, Max. I've been with you through thick and thin. And now, you're sidelining me for a fling?"

My patience is waning. "She's not a fling, Lawrence. And she's not just 'good' at it—she's great. Plus, I like having someone I trust taking care of these things. Look—I'm keeping you on retainer, and you're still getting the same hours. What's the issue?"

"That's a low blow," he hisses." After everything we've been through, you're questioning my loyalty? I want her off my territory, Max. I've cultivated these contacts, built these relationships. This Reebok deal? It's going to be my crowning achievement. My baby. And I won't let her or anyone ruin it."

His sense of ownership, the audacity, rubs me the wrong way. The guy's acting like I'm a piece of property he staked a claim on. "Look, Lawrence," I start, my voice cold and firm, "I don't owe you an explanation for my choices. As far as I'm concerned, you can take a break. Head back to Chicago for a bit."

Silence fills the line. When he speaks again, there's an icy venom in his tone. "You're making a big mistake, Max. You think you're on top of the world right now, but remember who helped you get there. You'll regret this."

The threat is clear, and I'm not one to be threatened. "Is that a threat, Lawrence?"

"Take it however you want." He spits back. The line goes dead.

I slide my phone into my pocket, my mood sinking further. Lawrence has always been territorial, but this is a new low. Even as these thoughts swirl, another one emerges, poking and prodding—what did he mean by "you'll regret this"?

I take a deep breath, letting the crisp evening air fill my lungs. Drama with Hailey, drama with Lawrence. Maybe I should've just stuck to slapping a puck around.

With a sigh, I decide to head back to the hotel. I've got a lot to think about.

33

Hailey

As I step into the Cedarwood Tavern, the sight of Max, lost in his own world, catches me off guard. There's something about him, hunched over his drink, that stirs a mix of concern and curiosity within me. Despite our recent tensions, I find myself relieved to see him, a fact I'm not quite ready to admit, even to myself.

"Mind if I join you?" I ask, my voice softer than I intend.

He looks up, clearly surprised, but manages a faint smile. "I mean, you're my fiancée. And you should probably lay a kiss on me too – keeping up appearances, after all."

Felt a little weird, but he was right. I plaster on a big smile and plant a kiss on his lips. He kissed me back, and more a moment, things are strangely normal.

I slide into the seat next to him, taking in his disheveled appearance. It's not like Max to look so... unguarded. We exchange hesitant small talk, the kind that dances around the edges of what we both really want to say. The air between us is charged with unspoken words and unresolved feelings.

"So," I venture cautiously, "How are you holding up with… everything?" I gesture vaguely, a reference to the suspension that hangs over him like a dark cloud.

Max sighs, swirling his drink absentmindedly. "It's been… tough, honestly. I should be on the ice right now, not stuck here figuring out damage control." He pauses, his gaze distant. "I feel like I'm benched in the most important game of my career."

His vulnerability strikes a chord in me. This is a side of Max I've rarely seen – the man behind the confident façade. "I can only imagine how frustrating that must be," I reply, my tone genuine.

"Yeah," he says, meeting my eyes. "It's like everything I've worked for is just… slipping away. And the worst part? I can't shake this feeling that I'm letting people down. My team, the fans, even the kids who look up to me."

His words reveal a depth of responsibility and concern I hadn't fully appreciated before.

"Max, you're doing what you can to make things right," I say, hoping to offer some comfort. "That's all anyone can ask for."

He gives a half-hearted chuckle. "I guess. It's just not where I expected to be, you know? I always thought I'd be remembered for my skills on the ice, not… this. Not my bullshit antics, not some engagement to set things right."

There's an honesty in his tone that tugs at my heart. For a moment, we sit in silence, the weight of his words hanging between us. It's clear that this suspension is more than just a temporary setback for Max. It's a challenge to his identity, his dreams, his very sense of self.

I want to say more, to delve deeper into his thoughts and feelings, but I hold back. We're still navigating this complex dance of our fake engagement, and I'm not sure how far I can push without crossing a line.

But as I sit there, watching Max grapple with his reality, I can't help but feel a newfound respect for him. Behind the confident, sometimes infuriating exterior, there's a man facing his vulnerabilities head-on. And in that moment, I see Max Decker not just as Cedarwood's hockey star, but as a person, flawed and real, just like the rest of us.

The silence stretches between us, a tangible thing, before I find the courage to delve deeper. "Max, if you don't mind me asking..." I begin, hesitating, "what was it like... growing up in foster care?"

Max's eyes flicker, a hint of surprise crossing his features. He leans back, his fingers tapping a rhythmic pattern on the bar. "I don't usually talk about it," he starts, his voice a mix of reluctance and something akin to relief. "My parents... they died when I was very young. Car accident."

I feel a pang of sympathy, imagining a young Max facing such a massive loss. "I'm sorry, Max. That must have been hard."

He nods, staring into his drink. "It was... chaotic. Moving from one home to another. Never really belonging anywhere." He chuckles, but there's no humor in it. "Always on the move, never letting anyone get too close."

Listening to him, the pieces start to fall into place. The cockiness, the bravado—it's all been a shield, a way to protect himself from the uncertainty and rejection he'd faced as a child.

"Hockey was my escape," he continues, his gaze distant. "On the ice, none of that mattered. It was just me and the game. It gave me a sense of control I never had anywhere else."

I watch him, seeing the passion in his eyes when he talks about his sport. It's more than just a game to him; it's a lifeline, a way to channel all the chaos of his early life into something positive.

"That makes a lot of sense," I say softly. "It's a part of who you are."

"Yeah," he agrees, a faint smile touching his lips. "It's the one thing that's always been there for me. The one thing I could count on."

His vulnerability in this moment is striking. The Max sitting beside me now is worlds away from the confident, often infuriating guy I've known. He's human, with scars and fears just like anyone else.

"I never knew," I admit. "I mean, I knew you were in foster care, but I didn't know how much it affected you."

Max shrugs, his guard coming back up slightly. "It's not something I broadcast. I learned early on that people treat you differently when they know your baggage."

I reach out, covering his hand with mine, wanting to offer some kind of comfort. "Max, we all have our baggage. It's what makes us who we are."

Max looks thoughtful for a moment before asking, "What about you? Being a lawyer and all. Do you like it?"

His question catches me off guard. It's rare for anyone to show genuine interest in that part of my life. "I do, actually," I respond, surprised by his curiosity. "There's something about the challenge of it, the strategy. I love diving into a complex case, untangling the threads. It's like solving a puzzle, and when you win, it's not just about victory. It's about making things right."

Max nods, listening intently. It feels nice, being asked about my work, about something that's a huge part of who I am.

"But," I continue, a wistful tone creeping into my voice, "in focusing so much on my career, I've let other parts of my life slip away. It's hard to believe how much time has passed since law school. Years already."

There's a pause, heavy with unspoken thoughts. The air between us feels charged, as if my last words have opened a door to a room full of memories and might-have-beens.

Max looks at me, his expression thoughtful. "Other parts of your life... you mean... like love?"

His directness takes me by surprise. I can feel my cheeks warm slightly, not sure how to navigate this turn in our conversation. "Yeah, I guess so," I admit, looking down at my hands.

There's a moment of silence, a mutual acknowledgment of the things we've given up, the sacrifices we've made. It's a strange sort of solidarity, understanding that we've both been so focused on our goals that other parts of life have been left in the shadows.

Max's gaze lingers on me, and I can't help but wonder what he's thinking. Does he feel the same way? Has he, too, sacrificed more personal aspects of his life for his career?

The weight of our unspoken feelings hangs in the air, a tangible thing between us. It's a delicate balance, this dance we're doing around the edges of what might have been and what could still be.

Max finally breaks the silence. "Life's about choices, I guess. We make them based on what seems right at the time. Doesn't mean we can't... find new paths, though."

His words are tinged with a hint of hope, a suggestion that perhaps it's not too late for either of us to explore those parts of life we've neglected.

"Yeah," I reply softly, feeling a small spark of hope myself. "New paths."

He looks at our hands, then up at me, and for a moment, I see gratitude in his eyes. "Thanks, Hailey. It... means a lot, you listening like this."

As we sit there, a new understanding dawns on me. Max Decker is a man shaped by loss and struggle, using humor and charm as armor against a world that's let him down more times than he cares to count. And in this moment, I feel closer to him than ever before, connected by the shared understanding of life's unpredictable twists and turns.

As Max finishes his drink, he sets the glass down with a finality that echoes the end of our conversation. "I need to clear my head," he says, standing up. "A walk might do me some good."

I nod, understanding his need for space. "Take care, Max."

He offers me a small, appreciative smile and a quick kiss before heading out into the night. I watch him go, feeling a complex mix of emotions. There's a warmth in my chest from the connection we've just shared, an understanding of Max I never had before. But it's tinged with frustration and a sense of incompletion.

Despite the deeper insights into his past, Max didn't touch on what happened between us in high school, the very thing that has been a thorn in my side for years. And then there's my own secret, the pregnancy, sitting heavy in my stomach. I'm not ready to share it yet, especially with so much uncertainty hanging in the air.

I sit there for a while, lost in thought, before deciding to leave. As I walk, I realize that while we've made strides in understanding each other, the path ahead is still murky. Our issues aren't resolved, and there's a part of me that's scared they never will be.

34

Max

As I wander aimlessly through Cedarwood's quiet streets, Hailey's words echo in my mind, mixing with my own thoughts. It's a strange feeling, this vulnerability. I'm Max Decker, the guy who always has a comeback, who doesn't let anything get too close. But tonight, with Hailey, I let down barriers I didn't even realize I had erected.

I find myself once more at the old hockey rink, the place where it all started for me. The cool air bites at my skin, but it's a welcome sensation, grounding me in the present. I sit on the bleachers, gazing out at the empty ice. It's here, in this sacred space of my youth, that I admit to myself something I've been avoiding: I care about Hailey. Deeply.

It's more than just our fake engagement or the shared history. It's her. Her resilience, her fiery spirit, the way she challenges me. I find myself wanting to be better because of her.

The idea of apologizing for the past gnaws at me. I should tell her I'm sorry for the way things ended between us in high school. But the thought is terrifying. What if bringing it up just makes things worse? What if it complicates whatever this thing between us is becoming?

My mind replays our recent moments together, the laughter, the shared looks, the unspoken understanding that seemed to be forming. And then there's the way she looked tonight, lost in thought, vulnerable yet strong. It's a side of Hailey I haven't seen before, and it draws me in even more.

I'm scared, not of the apology itself, but of what it could mean. What if she can't forgive me? What if she sees me as just that reckless kid from high school? The thought of losing this newfound connection with her, this fragile thing that's just starting to grow, is enough to twist my stomach into knots.

But as I sit there, alone with my thoughts, I realize something important. I need to make things right with Hailey, not just for her, but for myself too. I can't keep running from the past, from the things I've done. If there's a chance to fix it, to clear the air, I have to take it. It's the only way forward, the only way to potentially turn this fake engagement into something real.

The night grows colder, and I pull my jacket tighter around me. Hailey's image floats through my mind again, her smile, the way her eyes light up when she's passionate about something. It's comforting and yet confusing, stirring feelings in me that I haven't allowed myself to fully explore.

I stand up, resolve settling in. Tomorrow, I'll talk to her. I'll find a way to apologize, to start mending the bridges I burned years ago. It's time to face my fears, to face the possibility of rejection or pain, because the potential reward—having Hailey in my life, really in it—is worth the risk.

I head back towards the hotel, the weight of my decision heavy but empowering. I don't have all the answers, and I'm not sure how Hailey will react. But one thing is clear: I can't keep hiding behind jokes and charm. It's time to be honest, with her and with myself. The chapter closes on a note of determination, a silent promise to break the cycle I've been trapped in for too long.

35

Hailey

A FEW DAYS LATER, and my heart's thudding against my rib cage like a trapped bird. This isn't your typical Monday-morning jitters or pre-meeting nerves. This is me, Hailey, about to face the nation on "The Evelyn Davies Show."

"Stop biting your nails, Hales. Your fingers will be raw by the time the interview starts," Lucy chides from across my suite, where she's flipping through a magazine. Max rented me the suite across from his to give me a little privacy throughout our fake engagement. At that moment, I needed it—to pace like a mad-woman.

"I can't help it. What if I slip up? What if I accidentally let something slip?" I mumble, thinking of the secret I'm carrying.

She gives me a side-eye. "You're a lawyer. Keeping secrets is, like, your superpower."

I give a wry smile. "This isn't a courtroom. It's an entirely different ball game."

Lucy stands up, stretches, and walks over to me. "Okay, look," she begins, her voice a soothing lullaby, "Just breathe. In and out. You've faced scarier things than Evelyn."

"Name one."

Lucy ponders a moment. "That time in junior year when you accidentally ate that ghost pepper and thought you were going to die?"

I snort, laughing. "Oh God, that was awful."

Lucy grins. "See? This will be a walk in the park compared to that. Besides, Max will be with you. And no matter how much you two dance around each other, he's got your back."

I nod slowly, reassured. But a twist in my stomach reminds me of my secret. The one I haven't even shared with Lucy.

Lucy tilts her head, eyes narrowing. "Okay, spill. What's really going on? You've been jumpy all week."

I hesitate, my gaze flitting to the floor. "Promise not to freak out?"

She raises an eyebrow. "When have I ever freaked out?"

"Oh, only every time we watched a horror movie. Or saw a spider. Or—"

"Alright, alright! Point taken," she interrupts, chuckling. "Just tell me."

I take a deep breath, the words tumbling out faster than I can control. "I'm pregnant."

There's a beat of silence before Lucy's face splits into a wide grin. "Oh my God, Hailey! That's—Wait, WHAT?!"

"Yup. Surprise."

She blinks, seemingly trying to process the news. "But... but Max... and the engagement... and the PR stunt... and... BABY?!"

I wince. "Yeah, that about sums it up. And this goes without saying, but keep it to yourself!"

"I mean, duh!"

There's a knock on the door, causing both of us to jump. The door eases open, and Max pokes his head in, a look of casual confidence on his face. "Hey, they're ready for us. You good to go?" My eyes go wide at the sight of him, but nothing in his expression makes me think he heard Lucy's outburst.

I glance at Lucy, who's now trying her best to stifle her laughter, her hand covering her mouth. "Yeah," I reply, taking one last deep breath, "I'm good."

Max gives me a nod, clearly oblivious to our little secret-sharing session. "Alright, let's do this."

Lucy shoots me a wink as I follow Max out. If only he knew the storm that was coming. But for now, it's showtime.

"So, it's great to have you two with us today!" The lively voice of Evelyn Davies, everyone's favorite daytime talk show host, fills our hotel room. Her larger-than-life face beams from the enormous screen before us, her signature short, platinum hair perfectly styled as always.

"Thanks for having us, Evelyn," Max says smoothly, wrapping an arm around my shoulders. The Cedarwood skyline stretches out behind us, the twinkling lights of our lovely little town a testament to its charm.

"Can we just take a moment to appreciate that view?" Evelyn says, her eyes widening. "Cedarwood looks breathtaking!"

Max chuckles. "It's home. Has a special place in both our hearts."

Evelyn nods. "Speaking of hearts... Congratulations are in order! How does it feel to be engaged to your high school sweetheart?"

A pang of anxiety hits me. I glance at Max, hoping to ride his coattails through the answer.

He grins at Evelyn. "It's like rediscovering a part of myself I didn't know I missed. Hailey's always been special."

I melt a little inside, surprised by his heartfelt answer. "Max is... unforgettable," I reply with a smirk, "In both good and challenging ways."

Evelyn's eyes sparkle with mischief. "Max Decker, the NHL's poster boy for mischief and mayhem, now tamed by love. Who would've thought?"

Max chuckles, a playfully indignant look on his face. "Hey, I'll have you know I've always been an angel. It just took the right person to bring it out."

She raises an eyebrow, clearly amused. "An angel? Really?"

Max grins, winking. "Alright, alright, maybe more of a devil with good intentions. But like I said, all it takes is the love of a good woman." He pulls me close, placing a gentle kiss on my forehead. "And I've found the best."

Evelyn laughs. "Well, I must say, it's refreshing to see this side of you. Love suits you both."

I blush, feeling a little overwhelmed by the attention but also strangely proud of the man beside me. "Thank you, Evelyn. We're just taking it one day at a time."

Evelyn's laugh rings out. "Spoken like a true lawyer! Speaking of which, how's that been going, Hailey?"

"Can't complain. After all, what's a more natural pairing than an NHL star and a lawyer?" That gets a laugh out of Evelyn.

Max nods. "Having her by my side, both personally and professionally, has been a game-changer."

Evelyn leans forward, her gaze intense. "Any plans for the future? After the wedding, maybe?"

Max and I exchange a glance. He clears his throat. "We're taking things one step at a time. Right now, our focus is on the wedding."

I jump in, "And on enjoying our engagement."

Evelyn's warm smile stays fixed on her face. "Thank you for joining me," she says. But instead of the quiet pause of relief I'm expecting, both Max's and my phones start chiming incessantly. The air grows tense as the pings and vibrations create a chaotic symphony.

Max raises an eyebrow at me. "Are we suddenly that popular?"

Evelyn's eyes dart to our phones, then back to us, her grin stretching just a tad wider. It's clear she knows something we don't.

I excuse myself, pulling my phone from my clutch. My screen is flooded with notifications, texts, missed calls, and social media alerts. My heart drops as I open one of the articles being shared across every platform:

"Max Decker's Engagement a PR Stunt?"

Below the headline is a photo of Max and me from years ago, laughing and holding hands—an innocent picture, but with the context of the headline, it now looks damning.

Beside me, Max pulls out his phone, his face going pale. "Hailey..."

Evelyn, her finger pressed to her earpiece, is getting updated in real-time. Her sly grin tells us she's in the loop. "Well, it seems we have some breaking news. Care to comment on the recent rumors that your engagement is, in fact, a well-crafted PR move?"

Max steps in. "Whoever is spreading these rumors, they're wrong. This isn't some game to us."

Evelyn just tilts her head, that knowing smile still in place. "Is that right, Max? Hailey?"

I can feel the heat rising in my cheeks. "Interview's over," I say firmly.

Evelyn doesn't push further but does give a slight shrug. "Very well. Thank you for joining us, both of you."

As the screen goes dark, Max turns to me, his eyes blazing with fury. "What the hell, Hailey?"

I hold up my phone, showing him the articles and speculations. Pictures of us, snippets of conversations, and evidence of our well-constructed ruse are being displayed everywhere. His jaw clenches, and I can see the mix of anger and panic in his eyes.

Someone spilled it.

The only question was *who*.

36

Max

THE DUST FROM THE interview is still settling, the taste of shock and disbelief lingering in the air. The hotel suite is eerily silent except for the soft buzz from our phones, the digital world in an uproar over our faux-engagement revelation.

Hailey's eyes dart to me, wide and worried, "I think I might know who did this."

I raise an eyebrow. "Who?"

She swallows hard, clearly hesitating. "Lawrence." There's a tremble in her voice. "He confronted me after my doctor's appointment, warning me off your contracts. It seemed... more personal than just business."

I can't believe it. "That snake!" I growl, pulling my phone out and dialing Lawrence's number. It takes only two rings for him to pick up, his voice dripping with false sweetness. "Max! To what do I owe this pleasure?"

"Why did you leak the contract?" I bark, not in the mood for his games.

There's a brief pause, a drawn-out sigh, and then a low chuckle, "I thought it would be in your best interest, given how... inexperienced Hailey is."

I can feel my pulse pounding in my ears. "You did it out of jealousy!"

Lawrence snorts, "I did it because it's clear you're losing your edge, letting a pretty face influence your decisions."

"It's not about Hailey," I snap, clenching my free hand into a fist. "It's about you being a backstabbing weasel."

He chuckles again, more sinister this time. "Well, now that the cat's out of the bag, you're going to need my help more than ever."

"You think I'd trust you after this?"

Another pause, one filled with his damned smugness. "It would be in your best interest."

"Consider yourself fired, Lawrence," I seethe, my voice cold and final. "Don't contact me again."

I can picture his grin, even over the phone. "Good luck, Max. You'll need it."

As the line cuts off, I fling my phone onto the couch, fury coursing through me. Hailey reaches out, her hand warm and grounding against my arm. I look at her, her eyes full of sympathy, concern, and a hint of fear. We're in this mess together, and I have no idea how we're going to get out.

The room feels like it's charged with electricity, but not the good kind. A heavy, tense silence falls between us. Then, I, ever the one to use humor as a defense mechanism, quip, "Well, on the bright side, the world now knows we're officially back on the market."

Hailey's eyes narrow, her hands on her hips. "This is serious, Max! And you're making jokes?"

I shrug, trying to play it cool. "Sometimes, you gotta laugh to keep from crying."

She rolls her eyes, exasperated. "You always do this. Whenever things get serious, you just laugh it off. We're in a major mess, and all you can do is crack jokes!"

I raise an eyebrow, trying to lighten the mood. "Maybe if we sell tickets to the fake wedding, we could make some fake cash out of this?"

"Max!" she yells, frustration evident in her voice.

I can't help but be defensive. "What do you want from me, Hailey? To freak out? Is that going to help anything?"

She takes a deep breath, trying to control her temper. "I want you to take this seriously! I've put my career, my reputation on the line for this, and all you can do is make light of it?"

The truth is, I'm scared out of my mind. But letting her see that isn't in my playbook. "What's really going on here? Why are you so mad? This can't just be about the interview."

She hesitates, looking away, but then her gaze snaps back to mine, fiery and intense. "All my life, I've had to work twice as hard, be twice as good to be taken half as seriously. And now, this fake engagement stunt? It makes me look like a fool."

I'm taken aback, realizing this isn't just about the leak or even our pretend engagement. It's deeper.

"Hailey, I get it. But we're in this together, whether we like it or not."

She sighs, running a hand through her hair. "That's the thing, Max. I'm not sure if I want to be in this with you anymore."

I'm stunned, reeling from her words. "What are you saying?"

She looks down, her voice soft but firm. "Maybe it's time we end this charade. For good."

Eyes blazing, Hailey stands toe-to-toe with me. I've seen her fiery side before, but this is different. This is raw, unchecked emotion.

"I just thought..." I start, trying to sound calm and reasonable, "that maybe we could talk this out, find a solution."

She tilts her head, a sardonic smile playing on her lips. "You mean like how you 'talked out' our entire engagement without including me in the decision?"

Ouch. Point taken.

I run a hand through my hair, frustration evident. "Look, I get it, okay? It's a mess. But we can fix it."

She laughs, but it's devoid of humor. "You really don't get it, do you? It's not about the leak or the contract or any of that."

"Then what is it about?" I challenge, taking a step closer.

Hailey's voice drops to a whisper, her tone biting. "You. It's about you always making everything about you. You decide, you act, and the rest of us just have to deal with the aftermath."

I'm taken aback. That's... kind of true. But it's not what I want to hear right now. "Hailey," I say, trying to inject a little humor to diffuse the situation, "you know what they say about people in glass houses and throwing stones, right?"

Wrong move.

She stiffens, her gaze sharp and cold. "You might've fooled everyone else, Max, but not me. I thought you might've changed. Maybe grown up a bit. But you're still the same selfish prick you were back in high school."

And with that, she pivots on her heel and storms out of the room, leaving me in a daze of confusion and regret. I stare at the door long after it's closed, replaying the last few moments in my mind, trying to make sense of it all. The sting of her words, combined with the realization that maybe she's right, is a bitter pill to swallow.

My moment of introspection is cut short by the familiar chime of my phone. Pulling it from my pocket, I see Jake's name flash across the screen, followed by a succinct, Call me. Now.

Jake's never been one for mincing words, but even for him, this seems urgent. I take a deep breath, steadying myself. Hailey's words still echo in my mind, but I push them aside. I need to focus. And right now, that means dealing with the aftermath of our secret engagement being splashed across every tabloid and gossip site.

Tapping the call button, I mentally prepare myself for whatever comes next.

37

Hailey

I SIT ACROSS FROM my parents at our weathered wooden dining table, which has seen its fair share of family dinners, arguments, and everything in between. The swirling pattern on the wood seems to be the only thing keeping me grounded in this moment.

Taking a deep breath, I lean back in my chair. "So, that's it. The whole ridiculous story." My voice sounds way steadier than I feel.

As I sit with my parents, trying to wade through the mess of this engagement debacle, a heavy weight anchors itself in the pit of my stomach. The baby. My hand flutters instinctively to my belly, hoping they don't notice the brief gesture.

I ought to tell them, clear the air completely. But as I look into their concerned eyes, I can't bring myself to drop another bomb-shell tonight. They've absorbed enough shocks for one evening. Besides, I want to reveal it on my terms, when the moment feels right, and not as an additional footnote to this chaotic chapter.

Mom regards me carefully. "Sweetheart," she starts, a hint of concern in her voice, "I think the money and the business are the least of your problems right now."

I raise an eyebrow. I'd been so sure they'd be disappointed about not getting the financial relief we'd been banking on. "Really? Because from where I'm sitting, it looks like I've dragged our family's name through the mud for... well, for nothing."

Dad nods slowly. "It's not ideal, sure. But Hailey, you're our daughter. Money comes and goes, but your well-being. That's irreplaceable."

I blink back tears. "I just... I thought I was doing the right thing, you know? Saving the house, giving back to Cedarwood... and maybe, just maybe, proving to myself that Max could be different. That I could be different."

Mom reaches across the table, her fingers brushing against mine. "Honey, we can weather any financial storm. We've been through financial problems before, and we took care of those. This one will be no different. But seeing you so torn up, so... lost? That's what breaks our hearts."

I give a weak chuckle. "I guess fake engagements aren't exactly the path to self-discovery."

Dad smirks, the corners of his eyes crinkling with amusement. "Who'd have thought?"

The mood lightens a bit, and I can't help but let out a small laugh. "I just thought it'd be easy. A little playacting, some pretend kisses, then move on with our lives."

Mom tilts her head, a sly grin forming on her lips. "Pretend kisses? Oh, sweetie, I've seen you two together. That chemistry? That's not fake."

I groan, covering my face with my hands. "Mom, please."

She chuckles. "Just calling it like I see it."

I drop my hands, meeting her gaze. "It's just... complicated. Everything with Max always is."

Dad clears his throat. "Life rarely follows the plans we lay out for ourselves. But through all its twists and turns, you've always found your way, Hailey. You're stronger than you give yourself credit for."

I smile, warmth spreading through my chest. "Thanks, Dad. That means a lot."

"We love you," Mom says, her voice soft and full of emotion. "No matter what. And we're here for you, through thick and thin."

I nod, wiping away a stray tear. "I love you guys too. Thanks for always having my back."

After our chat, I find myself pacing my old room, my mind a whirl of thoughts and emotions. The posters from my teenage years that still adorn the walls are a stark reminder of simpler times. Back when the hardest decision was whether to go with skinny or flare jeans, and not dealing with the fallout of fake engagements gone awry.

I glance at my reflection in the mirror, memories of teen Hailey flashing before me. The one who doodled 'Mrs. Max Decker' on her notebooks and fantasized about that inevitable high school happy ending. But life, with its cruel twists, had other plans.

A soft knock on the door interrupts my musings. Before I can respond, the door eases open, revealing Lucy, her eyes wide with concern. "Hey, your parents let me in. You okay?"

I let out a weary chuckle. "Define 'okay.'"

She steps inside, closing the door behind her, and plops down on the bed, patting the space beside her. I join her, our shoulders touching, drawing comfort from her presence.

"Heard about the... fireworks with Max."

"God, I just... I feel so stupid. How the hell did I get into this situation with the last guy I should've?"

She smiles. "Because you weren't thinking of yourself—you were thinking of your mom and dad."

I snort, shaking my head. "I guess so."

"So, what are you going to do?"

"I... I don't know," I admit, running a hand through my hair. "I mean, it's not just about the fake engagement anymore. It's about us. About what I feel... and what I want."

Lucy tilts her head, regarding me with those wise, knowing eyes. "And what is that?"

I pause, swallowing hard. "I want him, Luce. But not like this. Not with secrets and lies between us."

She nods, her fingers finding mine and giving a gentle squeeze. "Then tell him. Lay it all out. No holding back."

"I'm scared," I whisper, my voice shaky. "What if he doesn't feel the same? What if it's all just been a game to him?"

Lucy sighs. "Max is many things, Hailey. But when it comes to you? I don't think he's playing games."

I bite my lip. "I need to see him. Face-to-face. Just... lay it all on the line."

Lucy's eyes sparkle with determination. "Then let's do it. No time like the present."

I stand, drawing a deep breath. "Okay. Let's go."

38

Max

"WHAT THE HELL WERE you thinking, Max?" Jake growls, tipping back a shot of whiskey and slamming the glass onto the counter. "Lying about something like that? And dragging Hailey into your circus?"

Sitting across from Jake in his dimly lit bar, the scents of aged wood and spilled alcohol permeate the air. Even without the weight of a long shift on his shoulders, Jake's glare has enough gravity to keep me in place.

I take a deep breath, the weight of the situation finally sinking in. "Look, Jake, it wasn't her idea—it was mine. And Hailey was all in not for the fame, the attention, or the money... but to save your parents' house. That's the only reason she agreed."

Jake chuckles, shaking his head in disbelief. "Sounds like her. Only Hailey would agree to such a harebrained scheme for a noble cause. I swear, that girl's heart is too big for her own good."

I let out a relieved chuckle, glad to see the hard edge in Jake's eyes softening. "Thanks for understanding, man."

He raises an eyebrow, fixing me with a stern look. "I didn't say I approved. I just said I understand. You two pulled a fast one on the whole town—hell, the whole damn planet. And while you might've had good intentions, it's not just about the two of you. Everyone's talking."

I groan, sinking deeper into my seat, knowing he's right. Cedarwood is a small place; news travels faster than wildfire. "I know, Jake. I know. I just... I thought it was for the best. But everything's gone to hell."

Jake sighs, leaning forward, his voice taking on a gentler tone. "Look, Max, Hailey's my sister. And I've known you long enough to see past your... antics. Let me talk to some people, set the record straight. Let them know why Hailey did what she did. They deserve to know."

There's a pause. There's something else I'm not saying, something I've been hiding from Jake for years. And there's something in those moments that make it impossible to hide any longer.

Jake's intense eyes bore into mine, searching for any trace of deceit or half-truths. It's like facing down a human lie detector.

"Alright, Max," Jake drawls, leaning back against the counter, crossing his arms. "Out with it. There's more you're not saying."

I shuffle my feet, suddenly feeling the weight of every misdeed I've ever committed. "Jake, promise me you won't punch me in the face, okay?"

He raises an eyebrow, a smirk playing at the corners of his mouth. "No promises."

Taking a deep breath, I start, "Back in high school... right at the end... Hailey and I... we, uh, had a thing."

Jake's smirk vanishes, replaced with a stone-cold expression. "What."

I rush to continue, knowing I'm walking a fine line. "Yeah, I know. Surprise, right? I never spoke about it because it was short-lived. At the time, I thought I was just into her because she was... well, Hailey. Smart, ambitious, beautiful."

Jake watches me, his expression inscrutable. "Go on."

"But seeing her again, after all these years... it's different now," I admit, my voice trembling with sincerity. "It's more than just a physical attraction. It's... everything about her."

I pause, gathering my thoughts. "She's brilliant, Jake. The way her mind works, the way she approaches problems, challenges... it's like watching a maestro conduct a symphony. And she's ambitious, never settling for anything less than what she believes she deserves. That tenacity is... it's intoxicating."

Jake leans forward, clearly interested in hearing more. "Keep going."

Taking another breath, I plunge in. "She's beautiful, not just on the outside, but inside too. The way she stands up for what she believes in, her good heart, the way she puts others before herself... it's so damned attractive. And let's not forget that stubborn streak. She's got fire, and she's not afraid to let it show."

I can't help the fond smile that tugs at my lips as I continue, "She challenges me, calls me out on my bullshit. With her, I don't feel like I have to be the always-confident Max. She sees right through me, and yet... yet she's still here, putting up with my crap."

Jake seems to consider this for a long moment before he finally speaks. "You love her, don't you?"

It's not a question. It's a statement. And as the weight of his words sinks in, I realize he's right.

"Yeah," I whisper, the realization hitting me like a ton of bricks. "Yeah, I really do."

Jake tilts his head, studying me with those all-knowing eyes of his. The silence between us stretches, the only sound the hum of the overhead lights and the distant chatter of the bar's patrons. After what feels like forever, he finally lets out a chuckle.

"You know, Max," he begins, shaking his head, "you can be a real shithead sometimes."

I grin, a mix of relief and mischief. "But I'm your shithead."

He laughs heartily at that, his earlier tension melting away. "Damn right. Look, we've been friends for what feels like a lifetime. And while I sometimes question my judgment for that, there's a reason I put up with your crap. Beneath all the cocky bullshit and swagger, you're actually a decent guy. Who would've thought?"

I feign surprise. "I'm offended you're only just figuring this out."

Jake leans in, his smile fading to a more serious expression. "All jokes aside, Max. You know you've got a punch coming, right? For not telling me about you and my sister, for all the sneaking around and secrets."

I tense up, mentally preparing for the blow. "I figured as much."

"But," he continues, holding up a finger, "there's one way you can avoid it."

"Oh?" I raise an eyebrow, intrigued.

He points a stern finger at me, his eyes locking onto mine. "Get your ass out of this booth, find my sister, and tell her how you truly feel. No games, no jokes, just pure, unadulterated truth. Because if there's one thing I know, it's that life's too short for missed chances."

I can't help the wide grin that breaks out on my face. "There's nothing I'd rather do."

Jake smirks, pushing me out of the booth. "Then go on, loverboy. Go get the girl."

39

Hailey

Downtown Cedarwood is shimmering with twilight, the buildings bathed in a soft glow. As I race toward the hotel, my heels clicking against the sidewalk, everything seems to blur into a mix of colors and sounds. My heart pounds in my chest, a mix of anxiety and anticipation.

And then, out of nowhere, there he is. Max. Racing from the other direction, a look of determination on his face. We stop, almost colliding, right in front of the Cedarwood Grand. The setting sun casts long shadows, and for a moment, it's like the world has stopped.

He grins, a little breathless, "Looks like you've got something on your mind."

I roll my eyes, but can't help the smile tugging at my lips. "Shut up, Max."

The momentary levity breaks, and a wave of emotion crashes over me. Taking a deep breath, I let it all out. "All these years, Max. That night, in high school. The way you just... left. You have no idea how much that hurt. I tried to move on, tried to pretend like it was nothing.

But being around you again, all these feelings just came rushing back. And I realized how much I've been carrying with me."

His face softens, and he takes a step closer. "Hailey, I—"

I shake my head, not letting him interrupt. "I need to get this out. I felt like you discarded me, like I was some disposable toy. I was furious with you, Max. I hid behind my anger, behind my pride. I convinced myself that I was over you, that I was past it all. But in these last few weeks, it's become clear. I can't just ignore it."

Tears form, blurring my vision. I'm not one for public meltdowns, but right now, in this moment, it feels like everything's crashing down. "Being close to you again, laughing with you, fighting with you... It brought back all those memories, all those feelings. And it hurts, Max. It hurts so much."

Before I know it, I'm wrapped in his arms, his familiar scent enveloping me. I bury my face in his shoulder, letting the tears flow. Surprisingly, it feels liberating. Like a weight I've been carrying for years is finally being lifted.

His voice is soft, filled with emotion, "I'm so sorry, Hailey."

I pull back slightly, looking into his eyes. "Why, Max? Why did you do it?"

He sighs, brushing a tear from my cheek. "There's so much I need to tell you. About that night, about everything. But first, I need you to know, it was never about you not being enough. It was me being young, stupid, and scared."

I take a deep breath, trying to process everything. Max's confession, my own feelings, everything that's happened. It's a lot to take in.

He takes my hand, his fingers entwined with mine. "Can we sit somewhere? Talk about everything?"

I nod, needing answers as much as he seems to want to give them. "Okay, Max. Let's talk."

The city lights are beginning to shine bright against the evening sky, setting the perfect backdrop as Max looks deep into my eyes. I can see the genuine regret there, mixed with a tinge of vulnerability that I've never seen from him before.

"First off," he starts, his voice uncharacteristically shaky, "I am so damn sorry for the way I treated you back then. I was an idiot, and I hurt you. There's no excuse."

I raise an eyebrow, feeling a surge of emotions coursing through me. "But?" I prompt.

He swallows hard. "But there's more."

I cross my arms, ready for whatever 'more' he's about to throw at me. "Alright then, out with it."

"If you think that I did what I did because you were just another notch on my belt, you're dead wrong, Hailey." His voice is filled with conviction, and I find myself taken aback.

I can't help the confusion that registers on my face. "What does that mean, Max?"

He takes a deep breath. "I ran from you because I was scared. Not because you were just a fling or some temporary diversion. In fact, it was quite the opposite."

My heart beats faster, my curiosity piqued. "Go on."

Max looks down, as if gathering his thoughts, before meeting my gaze once more. "When we got together back in high school, it was like everything I'd ever felt, every crush, every infatuation, it all paled in comparison. And that... that terrified me. So, I did what I always did back then—I ran. I ran from you, from what I felt, from everything that could have been."

I blink, processing his words. It's a lot to take in. Max Decker admitting to being scared? Of feelings?

"The truth is," he continues, his voice barely more than a whisper, "I love you, Hailey. I've loved you for a long time. Maybe even since we were kids. But I was too damn scared to admit it."

I feel tears sting my eyes, the weight of his confession pressing down on my chest. A whirlwind of thoughts cloud my mind, making it hard to form a coherent sentence. "Max, I..."

He places a finger on my lips, silencing me. "I know. I've said a lot. And I know words alone won't fix everything. But I needed you to hear it. The most important thing right now is, can you ever forgive me?"

My throat tightens as I process everything he's said. Can I forgive him? After all the pain and confusion? But then, looking into his sincere eyes, feeling the depth of his regret, and hearing the genuine love in his voice, it feels like maybe, just maybe, there's a chance for us.

I take a deep breath, my voice steadying as I speak. "Max, I need time. Time to process everything, to heal. But... I'm willing to try."

He exhales, relief evident in his face. "That's all I can ask for."

I can't help but tease Max with a smirk. "Well, there is something else you can ask for."

He raises an eyebrow, the playful glint in his eyes unmistakable. "Oh? And what might that be?"

"A kiss," I say, my tone sly, "But it's far from a given."

Max chuckles, the low sound reverberating in the still night air, "You should know by now, I've always been one to enjoy a challenge."

Without waiting for my reply, he leans in. Our lips meet, and it's like fireworks. All the pent-up emotions, the past misunderstandings, the undeniable attraction—everything culminates in this one passionate moment. The world around us blurs, and all that matters is the two of us, lost in each other.

After what feels like an eternity, we break apart, slightly out of breath but with matching grins on our faces. With a mischievous glint in his eye, Max takes my hand, leading me inside the Grand Hotel and towards the elevators.

The ride up is a blur of soft touches and whispered words. By the time we reach his floor, the anticipation is palpable.

Once inside his room, the atmosphere becomes electric. Max takes a moment to admire me, his gaze intense, making me blush. "You know," he starts, voice husky, as he begins to help me out of my dress, "seeing even just a hint of your bare skin is far more exciting than any adrenaline rush from the rink."

I laugh, pushing him lightly on the chest, "You always did have a way with words."

He smirks, slowly unbuttoning his shirt, "Only with you."

The room is filled with laughter and soft murmurs, as we continue to get more comfortable. Pieces of clothing are left discarded on the floor as we find our way to the bed, the outside world forgotten.

His fingers trail down my neck, a feather-light touch that sends shivers racing down my spine. With every passing second, the air in the room grows denser, filled with a potent mix of desire and anticipation.

"Did I ever tell you how much I adore your collarbones?" Max murmurs, leaning down to place a gentle kiss just above my clavicle. I let out a soft giggle.

"You and my collarbones? What an unexpected romance."

He chuckles, the sound deep and low. "Oh, but that's not all," he counters with a wicked grin. He traces a slow path down my arm, lips following suit, whispering praises for every inch of skin he discovers. "Your arms, so toned and yet so delicate, always held an allure."

His fingers and lips keep wandering, mapping out every curve and edge, from the hollow of my throat to the curve of my waist. I can barely keep up with his compliments.

"Your stomach," he continues, his fingers dancing around my navel, "it's perfect. Soft, yet strong. I could spend hours just admiring it." His voice is maddeningly tender, filled with genuine appreciation.

"Hours, huh? You sure have a lot of free time." I quip, unable to help myself.

He laughs, his warm breath tickling my ear. "Only for you."

My breath hitches as he continues his journey, praising my hips and thighs with words that make my heart race. By now, every touch feels electric, every kiss a spark that threatens to ignite me.

When he finally reaches my calves, he looks up with a smirk. "Always been a fan of these," he says, giving a playful squeeze. I arch an eyebrow.

"Really? My calves?"

He nods, his eyes filled with mischief. "Oh, absolutely. They're perfect. Every time you wore a sundress in high school, I just couldn't look away."

I burst into laughter, surprised by his unexpected admission. "You've always had an interesting taste."

He just grins, moving closer. "Only the best for me."

And then, he's back to teasing, fingers dancing along my inner thighs, making me gasp. The playful banter, the soft caresses, the passionate kisses—it's a heady mix, and I feel like I'm floating.

Just when I think I can't take any more of his maddeningly slow exploration, he stops. Looking deeply into my eyes, as if asking for permission. I nod, pulling him closer, letting him know without words that I'm more than ready for whatever comes next.

But Max, ever the tease, simply grins. "Patience," he murmurs, leaning down to capture my lips once more.

I groan in frustration, but there's a smile on my face. Because as maddening as he is, every second of this slow burn is utterly worth it.

The atmosphere between us thickens, turning from teasing playfulness to something deeper, something far more intimate. Max's fingers begin to explore, moving with a purpose, his touch growing more insistent, more intimate. His eyes never leave mine, watching me intently, searching for any signs of hesitation. But all he finds is an open invitation, my heart racing with anticipation.

The room is filled with our shared breaths, growing more erratic by the second. The sensations build, layer upon layer, bringing me closer and closer to the edge. His fingers work magic, finding all the right spots, pushing me to a place of pure ecstasy. The world blurs, narrowing down to just the two of us and the overwhelming waves of pleasure coursing through my body. With a final, shuddering breath, I succumb to the sensations, the release swift and powerful.

We weren't done. He moved over top of me, his manhood long and hard down below. He gazed down at me with those stormy, blue eyes, and I couldn't resist taking hold of him, wrapping my fingers around his thickness and guiding him inside.

I gasped as he pushes into me, my walls gripping him tightly, holding him inside. When he bottoms me out, he pulls back and drives in again, then again. I watch his muscles tense and flex, watch him vanish inside over and over. The pleasure builds and builds, my legs wrapped around him.

Even though in those moments it's nearly impossible to hold a thought in my head, one takes form nonetheless—we're making love, in the truest sense of the words.

Then he erupts inside of me, his body going stiff, the sensation of him climaxing bringing me over the edge. We rise together, then fall together. And then we're done.

Max pulls me close, our lips meeting in a deep, passionate kiss, tasting and savoring each other. He positions himself above me, looking deeply into my eyes. "Hailey Rogers," he whispers, his voice hoarse with emotion, "I love you."

I smile up at him, reaching up to tangle my fingers in his hair. "Max Decker, I love you too."

Afterwards, we lay intertwined, the soft sheets beneath us, the muted glow of the city lights filtering through the curtains. The full moon casts a silvery glow upon us, its light serene and peaceful. Max pulls me closer, his fingers tracing lazy patterns on my back.

As I drift off to sleep, nestled in Max's arms, the thought crosses my mind—how did a silly, fake engagement lead to something so deeply real? The universe certainly has a sense of humor. But one thing's for sure—while the beginning might have been based on pretense, what Max and I share now is the truest thing I've ever known.

Epilogue

HAILEY

THREE WEEKS FLY BY, and before I know it, I'm seated amidst a sea of roaring fans in a buzzing Seattle hockey stadium. Max? Oh, he's out there on the ice, living his dream as the Seattle StarPucks Center, and damn, is he bringing the heat or what? Every glide, every shot, every move is pure magic. I find myself caught up in the thrill of it all, even more than I'd ever imagined.

Lucy hollers from beside me, her new beau Sean at her side. "Who would've guessed you'd be the hockey girlfriend type?" she teases, nudging me with her elbow.

I chuckle, leaning into the moment. "Well, when the player's that hot, can you really blame me?"

Across from me, Jake throws a mock-stern glance in my direction. "That's my best friend out there you're ogling," he quips, a grin splitting his face.

Mom and Dad, cheer with gusto every time Max touches the puck. The pride evident in their eyes isn't just for their daughter's choice in men, but genuine appreciation for the player he is.

The last few weeks have been nothing short of a whirlwind. Max and I, from secret lovers to public headlines, have gone through it all. The town has watched, some with skepticism, others with joy, as our relationship unfolded. But amidst all the chaos, the heart of our love story remains untouched, strong, and true.

From the moment the truth of our 'fake' engagement spilled out to the world, there have been challenges. Contracts that fell apart, skeptical brands, and the ever-looming media scrutiny. But hey, Reebok stuck with Max. Go figure, they're total suckers for a real love story. And honestly, who could blame them?

Lawrence? He's old news, barely a blip on the radar now. After his treachery towards Max, word spread like wildfire in the tight-knit sports community. Let's just say his days of practicing law in the big leagues are as good as done. Maybe it's harsh, but karma has its way of catching up, and I'm not one to shed tears over someone who tried to stab the people I love in the back.

Speaking of love, Max's association with Reebok ended up being more of a blessing than we could've ever expected. They came through, honoring the charity package, and it was like a miracle for my family. The money was just what my parents needed to save their business, that precious legacy we'd been holding onto with every fiber of our being.

And true to form, Mom and Dad, ever the proud pair, insisted on paying back every dime to Max, though he was hardly in a rush to collect.

The past has a way of trying to cling to you, but I'm all about the now. My heart races in anticipation of the news Max and I are about to break during halftime. We've schemed, we've plotted, and it's going to be epic. But just as halftime arrives and I'm mentally prepping myself for our big reveal, Max throws a wrench in the plan.

He skates out to the center of the rink, alone, every eye in the arena on him. A bright spotlight hits him and he seems almost ethereal, otherworldly.

"Hailey!" he calls out, his voice echoing through the massive stadium. A hush falls over the crowd, and I'm stuck, my feet rooted to the spot. "I had this whole speech, you know? Something smooth, something suave. But damned if I'm not too beat for it. So here's the raw truth, no frills. Hailey Rogers, I love you. Every beautiful inch of you."

And then, before I even have a chance to catch my breath, he's down on one knee. My eyes are drawn to the gigantic screen overhead, magnifying every detail, and there it is. The antique ring I'd pointed out on a lazy stroll through downtown, never in a million years thinking it'd be wrapped around my finger. My heart does a funny little jive in my chest. The past, present, and future blur together in a beautifully chaotic whirlwind.

The weight of thousands of eyes on me should be intimidating. But by now? I've grown rather used to it. Without hesitation, I scream out a joyful "Yes!" into the echoing stadium, sending the crowd into ecstatic frenzy.

Turning to my family, I shout, "Hold it up when I'm down there!" Determination in my steps, I hurry down to the side of the rink and slip on a pair of ice booties—something you learn as a hockey girlfriend to always carry—over my shoes. It's time for my own bit of mischief.

I make my way to the center of the rink, each step filled with purpose. "Thought you were the only one with surprises up your sleeve?" I challenge Max with a cheeky grin.

At my signal, my family unfurls a massive banner. Bold, block letters proclaim, "Congratulations, Dad!" accompanied by the drawing of a comically cute cartoon baby.

I see the moment it clicks. Max's eyes, so sharp and focused just moments ago, widen in surprise. A second passes, then another. Then, with a triumphant roar, he pumps his fist into the air and shouts, "Hell yes!"

Drawing me into his arms, we share a kiss amidst the roaring approval of the crowd. We're surrounded by thunderous applause, flashing lights, and shouts of joy. Yet, in that moment, it's just the two of us—our hearts aligned, united by love and a shared future.

THE END

***

A NOTE FROM THE AUTHOR

Dear Reader,

Thanks for choosing my book! I hope you enjoyed Max and Hailey's journey. Please consider sharing your thoughts with a review on Amazon—your feedback not only helps others find their next favorite book but also means a lot to me.

Now some exciting news! If you liked 'Pucking My Fake Fiance' you will love '***Pucking My Bad Boy Boss***.' It's up next! Keep reading for a sneak peek.

Thanks again for being a part of this journey.

Love,

Livvy

Scan this QR code to get your copy of 'Pucking My Bad Boy Boss':

I never thought that ridiculously hot one-night-stand would end up being my grumpy boss.

It started when I locked eyes with a mysterious stranger, and it should have ended after our fiery encounter.

Years later, managing my brother's hockey team is a dream come true...

...Until I met my new boss.

The gorgeous man from my past is now the team's owner—and my brother's best friend.

Dominic "Dom" Steele. Owner of an impressive sports empire in the U.S.

At 6' 3", his presence is commanding. Each muscle finely sculpted, his body is pure perfection.

Unable to deal with the undeniable chemistry, I accept a job offer from a rival team.

To appease his investors, he proposes a deal to benefit both our teams: a fake engagement.

Our game brings us closer... ...and blurs the lines between fantasy and reality.

Stuck together in a small cabin when a blizzard hits, we relive our electrifying connection.

And now I'm pregnant.

I'm falling for him.

But will he put his ambition aside to be the daddy my baby deserves?

Scan this QR code to get your copy of 'Pucking My Bad Boy Boss'!

Scan me

A Sneak Peek is just one page away.

Pucking My Bad Boy Boss

An Enemies to Lovers Fake Relationship Romance

SNEAK PEEK

1

Isabella

"Jenna, these conferences could put a caffeine-addicted squirrel to sleep," I groan into my phone, swirling the olive in my martini. 'Neon Nights' is humming with the seductive energy of New York City nightlife. A deep blue glow casts an almost dreamlike haze over the hip crowd, and the bar's modern aesthetics provide the perfect contrast to my day at the impossibly dreary NHL Annual Strategy Symposium.

Laughter dances from the other end of the call. "I can't even picture you, Miss Always-in-Control, at one of those things. All suits, ties, and puck dynamics. But come on, it can't be *that* bad?"

I roll my eyes, even if she can't see it.

"Imagine getting mansplained about the aerodynamics of hockey sticks," I say with a hint of dry humor. My feet ache in my high heels, longing for the comfort of my usual sports attire.

Jenna's laughter rings through the space. "I bet you were wearing your 'thoroughly unimpressed' face the whole time," she teases.

"Oh, absolutely," I reply. "But I'm really not a fan of this whole suit-and-heels thing. My feet are staging a full-on rebellion."

"Missing your comfy sneakers, aren't you?" Jenna asks knowingly.

"You have no idea," I groan. "And don't get me started on the hair. This power bun has been a nightmare." I reach up, letting down the tight bun that's been pulling at my scalp, and my hair cascades down in a wave of liberation.

Jenna chuckles. "Ah, the small joys of shedding the professional armor and coming back to your true self."

"Exactly," I agree, running my fingers through my hair. "Give me my team jacket and a pair of comfortable shoes any day. That's the real Isabella Carrington, not this suited-up, high-heel-enduring version."

"Well, suit or no suit, you're still the Isabella who's kicking ass and taking names," Jenna says supportively.

"Thanks, J."

As I vent, my gaze drifts across the bar, landing on a sight that stops me mid-sentence. There's a man, all sharp lines and brooding intensity, seated in a way that screams confidence. The tailored cut of his suit showcases broad shoulders and an athlete's physique. The dim lights catch the intricate tattoos that wind down his rolled-up sleeve on his left arm all the way to his hand, then back up along the same side of his neck, revealing tales I can only guess at.

"Earth to Izzy!" Jenna's voice snaps me back to reality.

Caught in my open admiration, I quickly divert. "Sorry, Jen. Just... surveying the room."

"Ooh, someone caught your eye?" Her voice lifts with mischief.

I smirk, keeping my voice casual while my gaze subtly follows the man across the bar. "Just a random guy. He's definitely hot, but I've got bigger fish to fry."

Jenna laughs. "Always business with you. Speaking of which, why'd you call?"

I sigh, tapping my nails against the bar. "Needed a break, and a momentary escape. But you know me, always finding a way to work."

Jenna's laughter rings through the phone, light and teasing. "Seriously, give me *one* good reason why—" There's a sudden pause, a muffled sound, then Jenna's tone shifts, more serious. "Oh, shoot, that's Dr. Reynolds calling from the hospital. Might be important. I gotta take this. Keep me posted, okay? And go conquer the world, or at least that bar."

"We'll see. Bye, Jen" I end the call, laying my phone on the bar. Fishing a sleek tablet from my bag, I pull up a few documents, figuring I can squeeze in some work while enjoying my drink. Then it's back home to Seattle in the morning.

I lose myself in reports and strategies, making notes and planning moves for my team, the Silver Blades. In the periphery of my vision, I occasionally notice the tattooed stranger glancing my way, his dark eyes intense. But right now, my focus is all on the game off the ice. After all, in the fast-paced world of sports management, every moment counts.

I don't know what hits me first—the potent warmth of the martini or the sultriness in the gaze of the tattooed man. It's a heady combination. I'm used to feeling eyes on me, especially in my line of work, but this? This is a different ballgame—or hockey game, in my case.

I glance up, just a cursory survey, but I'm not prepared for what greets me. Those intense eyes, exuding a primal, unspoken challenge. It's the kind of confidence you don't often see, the kind that says he's played the game—in more rinks than one—and knows how to win. That hint of a smirk, so infuriatingly arrogant, is enough to send a jolt straight to my core.

There's something else, too. The guy looks *familiar* in a way I can't quite place.

My cheeks flame. *Damn it, Carrington, pull yourself together.*

I quickly return my attention to the screen, telling myself that the bar's ambient temperature is the reason for my sudden warmth. I become engrossed in a particularly gnarly contract clause, letting its jargon and complications distract me from the man who seems to have temporarily short-circuited my brain.

A new email pops up, pulling my attention. Some update about the Seattle StarPucks, the newest franchise team to hit the ice. As I scan the lines, I make a mental note to respond later. My eyes flit over stats, percentages, margins—numbers and figures that ground me, making the world make sense again.

Around me, the bar comes alive. Glasses clink, laughter grows louder, and the sensual beats of 'Earned It' by the Weeknd begins to play. The seductive rhythm weaves through my consciousness, adding a layer of sultriness to the mundane data before me. And yet, even amidst all this, I can feel the weight of a particular gaze.

Resisting the temptation becomes a game. How long can I keep my focus strictly professional with the embodiment of temptation mere feet away? The more I dive into my work, the more my surroundings blur into indistinct chatter, shadows, and light.

The bustling hum of the bar, the background music, it's all become a comforting white noise. I lose myself in the drudgery, each line blurring into the next.

"You know, they say puck size matters," a voice rumbles suddenly, low and tinged with mischief, breaking through my trance.

Startled, I almost knock over my martini, catching it just in time. I slowly lift my eyes from my screen. No longer across the room, the mysterious stranger is now leaning against the bar beside me, all broad shoulders and simmering intensity. The close proximity sends a jolt of awareness down my spine. The heat he gives off is palpable, like standing too close to a bonfire.

"Excuse me?" I challenge, arching an eyebrow, my voice dripping with feigned disdain, though my racing heart gives away my surprise.

His lips curve into a teasing grin, blue-green eyes dancing with amusement. "Just reflecting on a topic from the conference today. Interesting how such minute details can have such a significant impact on the game."

My cheeks blaze as realization dawns. He'd been at the Strategy Symposium too. No wonder he'd looked so familiar.

And yet, it's the man himself that truly captures my attention. Up close, his charm is practically an assault. Those expressive eyes, the texture of his short beard, his laugh lines—it's all intensely, impossibly distracting. And I've never been a tattoo sort of woman, but the way those designs look crawling up his ropey, thick forearm, vanishing underneath the tightly-rolled sleeve of his shirt, reappearing up above along his thick neck... *damn*.

As he starts to introduce himself, holding out a hand, I cut him off, "Dominic Steele. You're Dom Steele." The words spill out, the dots finally connecting. He's not just some hockey enthusiast; he's THE hockey legend.

That's why he looked so familiar. Not just because he was some guy who happened to be at the conference, but that he was a hockey god in the flesh!

For a split second, I feel like a rookie who's stepped onto the ice for the first time, disoriented and off-balance. The man beside me isn't just a handsome stranger; he's a monumental figure in the world of hockey, a living legend. And here I am, working on budget reports and getting tipsy in his presence.

A touch of pink colors my cheeks, but if he notices my embarrassment, he doesn't show it. Instead, with the smooth grace of someone who's been in the limelight for years, he replies, "Most people just call me Dom."

I'm too stunned to speak.

He gestures to the empty seat beside me. "Mind if I join you? I promise I won't critique your spreadsheet. Much."

His teasing tone, combined with that signature Dom Steele confidence, is utterly captivating. All I can manage is a sassy smirk as I motion for him to take the seat. Work can wait, but opportunities like this? They're as fleeting as a puck in the final seconds of a tied game.

"Go ahead," I say, trying to sound cool and in control. Still, my voice hitches just slightly, and inwardly I'm berating myself for it. The bar's ambient murmur seems to fade a touch as he settles next to me. I nod to the seat beside mine, a clear invitation.

Watching Dom move is like observing poetry in motion. For a guy built like a fortress, he carries an unexpected grace with every step. It's a strange juxtaposition—the raw power of an athlete combined with the fluidity of a dancer. As he takes the seat, there's a smooth pivot, an ease in his descent, the lean of his tattooed arm on the bar counter.

My eyes can't help but drift down, taking in the defined muscles of his forearms, and then, a bit lower, to his perfectly shaped behind. A playful, albeit inappropriate thought crosses my mind: I wonder what those arms would feel like wrapped around me—and just how firm that amazing butt really is, what it'd feel like bare underneath my hands...

Whoa, Isabella! Get a grip! But oh, what a deliciously sinful grip that could be.

"So, you were at the conference too?" I ask, hoping to steer my thoughts to safer territory.

Dom chuckles, his smoldering intensity momentarily replaced by amusement. "Yep, and it was every bit as riveting as watching paint dry."

I snort with laughter, nearly spitting out my drink. "Thank God I wasn't the only one stifling yawns! I thought I was going to be buried under PowerPoint slides."

His laughter is hearty and infectious. "And let's not even get started on those long-winded keynote speeches."

We exchange playful banter, tearing apart various elements of the conference, and it's evident we're on the same wavelength. It's surprisingly easy, this back and forth with him.

Dom arches an eyebrow, his magnetic eyes twinkling with mischief. "Anyway, did you catch that session on the evolutionary trajectory of the hockey puck? I mean, who knew there was a prehistoric age for those little rubber discs?"

I stifle a giggle. "Oh, absolutely enlightening! I was on the edge of my seat. And don't even get me started on the dramatic unveiling of the new puck design. I've never seen so much fanfare over a few added grooves."

He laughs, a rich, hearty sound that has a flutter running down my spine. "Oh, come on! That laser light show? The dramatic music? It was like witnessing the launch of a new iPhone—just rounder and... more slappable."

I feign a dramatic gasp. "How dare you! Pucks are the very essence of our sport! Next, you'll be making fun of the strategic placement of water bottles on the bench."

He leans in conspiratorially, voice dripping with mock gravity. "Ah, now that's classified info! But between you and me, I've always believed there's a secret society deciding the precise angles those bottles should face. I mean, it's the only logical explanation."

My laughter is genuine and unbridled. It feels like a release, especially after the stiffness of the conference. "Oh, please. It's all about the optimal squirt trajectory."

Dom chuckles, clearly delighted by my response. "Ah, squirt trajectory. Now that's a panel discussion I'd sign up for!"

There's a lull in the conversation, and right away I notice that it's not an awkward pause—not even a little. It's the kind of pause you have with someone you've known for a while, someone you're totally comfortable with.

Strange, considering I've just met the man.

"So, Isabella," Dom leans in, his voice dropping a notch, "what do you do when you're not suffering through tedious conferences? You mentioned the Silver Blades earlier."

"Ah, the Silver Blades," I say, pride evident in my voice. "I'm their Strategy Manager. I pretty much oversee the strategic planning and execution for the team. Makes me sound important, right?"

Dom's eyes light up with genuine interest. "That's impressive. Not just a pretty face then?" The flirtation is evident, but it's his playful tone that makes me laugh rather than roll my eyes.

"I like to think I have the brains to match," I retort, shooting him a sassy grin.

I can't ignore the electricity in the air, the tingling sensation whenever our hands brush, or the heat that rises in me every time I catch his gaze. It's been ages since I've had this much fun talking to someone, and for a fleeting moment, I forget who he is—forgetting the fame, the accolades, and the legacy.

For now, in this dimly lit bar in New York, he's just Dom. And I'm having the time of my life.

2

Dom

"I swear, if one more person tries to explain to me the aerodynamics of a slap shot, I might just spontaneously combust," I say, grinning devilishly.

Isabella throws her head back, laughing. "Oh, come on, Dom. Surely, after all these years on the ice, there's some hidden, profound mystery about it you've missed?"

I smirk, leaning closer. "The only mystery here is how I've managed to stay awake through half those sessions."

Her laughter gradually fades, and I take the moment to really look at her. Damn. Up close, she's even more striking. The dim bar lights catch the rich, raven-black strands of her shoulder-length hair, making them shimmer like the midnight sky. Her hazel eyes, framed by those sleek, black cat-eye glasses, have this intense yet playful glint.

It's as if they're challenging me, daring me to keep up with her sharp wit.

Her laugh, that genuine, soul-deep laugh, makes her entire face light up. The way her lips curve, full and inviting, has my mind wandering down paths it probably shouldn't. And it's not just her face. I can't help but appreciate her lean athletic frame, the unmistakable curves that her tailored pantsuit hints at. She has me wondering how those toned muscles would feel under my hands.

She's a blend of strength, beauty, and intelligence. It's a dangerously alluring combination.

"So, Isabella," I begin, my voice dropping an octave lower, involuntarily adding a sultrier tone. "Strategy Manager for the Silver Blades, huh? Sounds important. Do you, like, plan out how many left turns players make during a game?"

She snorts, her earlier laughter replaced with an amused smirk. "Oh, at least a hundred. It's a very scientific process. Mostly involves me spinning a wheel and yelling out directions."

I chuckle, leaning back and taking a sip of my drink. "I knew it! All those years wondering about the secret strategies, and it's just a glorified game of Twister."

She laughs again, and I'm caught in the melodious sound. I'm used to being the charmer, the one who has people hanging on his every word. But here, with Isabella, it feels like the tables have turned. Every quip, every laugh, every glance she throws my way—I'm hooked. And it's a feeling I'm not quite sure what to do with.

I let the moment linger, the atmosphere thick with playful tension. There's a magnetic pull between us, undeniable and strong. It's been a long time since I've felt this kind of connection, especially so instantly.

"So," I start, leaning my elbow on the bar counter, "how does some-one like you end up in hockey management?"

She arches a perfectly sculpted eyebrow, her smirk growing more pronounced. "Someone like me? You mean a woman?"

I can't help but laugh, that smooth, self-assured chuckle that's gotten me out of more than a few tight spots. "Nah," I reply, my eyes shamelessly raking over her, "more like a *beautiful* woman. Someone who looks like you wouldn't have to work a single day in your life... unless you wanted to."

For a split second, I worry I might've laid it on too thick. But then, a delicate blush spreads across her cheeks, making her already stunning face glow. God, I could get addicted to that blush.

She rolls her eyes, though the smile tugging at her lips gives away her amusement. "Oh, please. That's your go-to line, isn't it? Well, for your information, Mr. Steele," she playfully stresses my name, "my love for hockey strategy isn't rooted in my looks. It started with my brother."

I raise an eyebrow in genuine curiosity, my previous cockiness momentarily overshadowed. "Your brother?"

She nods, taking a sip of her drink. "Mhm. He was obsessed with hockey. Played it all through school and college. I never really had the inclination to get on the ice myself, but I was always there, watching his games. The more I watched, the more fascinated I became with the strategies, the planning, the maneuvers. Not the physical side of the game, but the mental one."

Leaning in closer, her enthusiasm palpable, she continues, "I started seeing patterns, predicting plays before they happened. And when my brother moved on to a minor league, I began suggesting strategies. Turns out, I had a knack for it. From there, it was just a short leap to the management side of things."

She finishes her tale, looking a touch bashful. It's a new side to her, one that intrigues me even more. "So, you're the brains behind the operation," I muse aloud, genuinely impressed.

She shrugs modestly, but her eyes gleam with pride. "Someone's got to do the thinking, right?"

Chuckling, I nod in agreement. "True that. Many guys I know just skate around, hoping for the best. But I always believed in the power of a good strategy."

Her face lights up, pleased with the validation. "Exactly! It's an art, a game of wits. It's what makes it exciting."

As the night wears on, the atmosphere between us lightens, making it easy to forget the outside world. It's her turn to probe now.

"So, Dominic," she drawls out my name teasingly, the soft glow of the bar lights making her eyes dance, "I've always been curious. After such a legendary stint on the ice, where did you vanish to?" Her playful tone falters slightly, "Of course, I mean after... the injury."

Instantly, her cheeks redden, as if realizing she may have overstepped. "Sorry, I shouldn't have brought that up."

I wave off her concern, the memories of that day, though painful, having been dealt with a long time ago. "It's alright, Isabella. Ancient history." I lean back in my chair, the leather creaking softly under my weight. "You know, life has a funny way of pushing you in the direction you're meant to go. Sometimes it's a gentle nudge, other times it's a shove off a cliff. Either way, I believe it all happens for a reason."

She seems taken by my response, her tense shoulders relaxing. A smile graces her lips, one that seems both relieved and genuinely pleased. "That's a refreshing attitude," she remarks.

Under the table, my fingers drum a nervous rhythm. Few people know about my recent endeavors in the hockey world. I've been working in the shadows, letting others take the limelight. And while part of me wants to spill everything to Isabella, a gut feeling tells me it's not the right time. Some secrets need to remain hidden, at least for now.

However, it's as if she reads my mind. Her gaze sharpens, eyes narrowing playfully, "What are you hiding, Mr. Steele? You have that look. The one people get when they're sitting on a juicy piece of gossip."

Caught off guard, I'm saved by the bartender's timely announcement, his voice echoing through the now almost-empty establishment. "Last call, folks!"

She shoots me a mischievous glance, leaning in as if to share a secret, her lips just inches from my ear. "You got lucky this time, Dom. But I have a knack for uncovering secrets." Her warm breath sends shivers down my spine.

Pulling away with a smirk, she collects her things, ready to call it a night. And as she does, I can't help but think that life's little push tonight was leading me right to her.

As the atmosphere between us thickens, the pull becomes undeniable. In a bold move, I reach over and slide my hand onto her thigh, feeling the warmth of her skin even through the fabric of her dress. Our eyes lock, and for a moment, everything else blurs.

"You said you've got a knack for uncovering secrets," I murmur, my voice dripping with intent. "What else are you good at uncovering?"

A coy smile dances on her lips, and the glint in her eyes tells me she's picked up on my challenge. "Wouldn't you like to know?"

The next thing I know, we're rushing towards the elevators, barely able to keep our hands off each other. The world outside is a distant echo as our mouths collide, every touch a promise of the fire that's about to ignite.

Scan this QR code to keep reading 'Pucking My Bad Boy Boss'!

Scan me